Mount Athos and Meteora: The History of Became Orthodox Christian

By Charles River Ed

David Profter's picture of Mount Athos

About Charles River Editors

Charles River Editors is a boutique digital publishing company, specializing in bringing history back to life with educational and engaging books on a wide range of topics. Keep up to date with our new and free offerings with this 5 second sign up on our weekly mailing list, and visit Our Kindle Author Page to see other recently published Kindle titles.

We make these books for you and always want to know our readers' opinions, so we encourage you to leave reviews and look forward to publishing new and exciting titles each week.

Introduction

Mount Athos

A picture of the area around Vatopedi monastery

"Clear water where evergreens, azaleas cool ceremoniously...a kele lost among cedars, its roof open to eagles, door unhinged...silver leaves like a congregation of spiders..." When one hears these enchanting descriptions, from poet David Posner's 1964 composition "Mount Athos," it is not difficult to understand why this sleepy paradise is often extolled as the most peaceful and private corner of Greece, if not all of Europe. Mount Athos is the easternmost finger of the Halkidiki peninsula – a mountainous sliver of land that stretches about 37.3 miles long and 4.3-7.5 miles wide, with a surface area of about 150 square miles. Towering over the tightly-packed chestnut forests and the blue, crystalline waters of the Aegean Sea at a height of 6,670 feet is the snow-dusted crest of the mighty mountain itself.

Known to the locals as *Agion Oros*, or the "Holy Mountain," the peninsula today is most famed for its exclusivity, a place that continues to bar all women and their daughters from entry. The fortress-like monasteries scattered amongst the slopes and the clusters of cells clinging to the cliffs are occupied by monks of the Eastern Orthodox Church. Of course, its male-only population is just one aspect of the peninsula's anomalous nature.

Planted on the peninsula's coast is a black Byzantine Cross, a flat, cross-shaped monument with a trinity of flared, wide-armed, Greek crosses in place of its arms and a traditional Christian cross in its center, kissed with rust. It serves as an emblem of the monastic society that resides there, and it delineates the boundary between Mount Athos and the rest of Greece. Entering this hallowed peninsula is like setting foot into a living time capsule, because life here has not changed in well over 1,000 years. Mount Athos is one of only two places on earth (the other being the Mar Saba) that chooses to run on "Byzantine time," meaning Hour 0:00:00 only begins at sundown. Moreover, it is the only territory in the world that flies the Byzantine flag, a regal, sword and cross clutching double-headed eagle set against a rippling canvas of gold.

Of course, to reduce Mount Athos to an antediluvian, single-sex monastic retreat would be an oversimplification of the fascinating history and simple, yet complex culture that has developed on this stunning strip of land. This is a place as mystically mysterious as it is serene, a space abound with treasures, miracles, and spiritual revelations. But for a place where purity and God-fearing devotion apparently reign supreme, it is certainly burdened with its fair share of controversy.

Meteora

Dennis David Auger's picture of Meteora

The Tower of Babel is arguably among the most well-known allegories of the Old Testament. As told by the Book of Genesis, the story revolves around a post-flood batch of Noah's descendants who dwelled in Babylon's Mesopotami, a city erected by King Nimrod. The population multiplied rapidly over the years, and the city's inhabitants fostered the growth of their culture and enhancing the infrastructure of their territories, made easier by the existence of only one common language. Naturally, the pride of the Mesopotamian residents burgeoned, but their contentment, poisoned by their greed and ambition, began to decline. The only way to prevail over this slump, believed a particularly enterprising group of individuals, was to construct a colossal ziggurat (a "rectangular, stepped tower") that would ascend past the clouds and into the heavens. With this tower, they intended to "make a name for" mankind and the untouchable abilities of mere mortals, thereby severing their relationship with God their Creator for good.

According to the Bible, God was far from impressed, and to add insult to injury, the architects behind this attempt deliberately opted for man-made materials, such as brick and tar, rather than stone, timber, and other natural building blocks gifted to them by God. The overblown pomposity and conceit of His subjects had to be ceased at once, lest they stray further away from Him. Thus, as the people slept, God reached down and scooped up handfuls of the slumbering Mesopotamians and strewed them across the continents, creating 70 different nations and tribes. When they awoke, the bewildered residents of the newly birthed nations were speaking in different tongues. With the architects scattered around the globe and now unable to understand one another, construction of the partially built ziggurat came screeching to a halt. It was later dubbed the "Tower of Babel," or the "Tower of Confusion." This miserable monument, which served as a haunting reminder of man's subservience to God, was continuously marred by fire and battered by the elements over the years until it eventually crumbled back into the earth.

Close to 1,850 miles to the west of Babylon, roughly 3,000 years later, yet another group of mere mortals set out on a daring, but seemingly fragile quest to build their homes in a place that – at the very least – symbolically neighbored the Kingdom of God. Evidently, these mortals had earned the Lord's blessings, for there, a smattering of their descendants remain to this day. Contrary to the builders of Babel, these God-fearing venturers constructed these dwellings with the purpose of wholly devoting their lives to the Lord. More admirable yet, these dwellings were not lofty towers that took dozens of years to assemble, nor were they built atop solid ground; instead, they ranged from small huts to compact complexes perilously perched atop and embedded into the nooks and fissures of stone mountains. This forest of jagged stone pillar, which looms over gorgeous valleys and a lush, densely forested stretch of land, is none other than Meteora, situated in the quaint town of Kalabaka in the northwestern part of Thessaly, Greece.

Mount Athos and Meteora: The History of the Greek Landmarks that Became Orthodox Christian Monasteries looks at the unique regions and what life has been like there since ancient times. Along with pictures depicting important people, places, and events, you will learn about Meteora and Mount Athos like never before.

Mount Athos and Meteora: The History of the Greek Landmarks that Became Orthodox Christian Monasteries

About Charles River Editors

Introduction

   Ancient History

   The Rise of the Rock Pillars

   The First People of Meteora

   The Byzantine Era

   Endless Battles

   The Floating Monasteries of Meteora

   Fascinating Friars

   The Modern Era

   Meteora in the Modern Era

   Online Resources

   Meteora Bibliography

   Mount Athos Bibliography

Free Books by Charles River Editors

Discounted Books by Charles River Editors

Ancient History

"The man who follows Christ in solitary mourning is greater than he who praises Christ amid the congregation of men." – attributed to St. Isaac the Syrian

Fittingly, Mount Athos has long been considered by nearby residents, well before it was dominated by the Christian faith. Prior to the birth of Christianity itself, the peninsula was known as "Akte." It was only after the fateful episode starring the Thracian *gigante* Athos, as local legend dictates, that this formerly flat countryside was given its name.

Once upon a time, a terrible brawl erupted between the Thracian Giants and the Olympians, the former led by Athos, and the latter headed by Poseidon, god of the sea. In the midst of the tussle, Athos hoisted an enormous hunk of rock (soon to be the peak of Mount Athos) and flung it at Poseidon, but the mass narrowly missed its target and crashed into the sea, eventually forming the grand mountain seen today.

A conflicting version of this tale credits Poseidon for being responsible. In this account, it was the sea god who lobbed the hunk of rock at Athos. Unfortunately for Athos, Poseidon was evidently the better shot, for the peak landed atop his opponent, burying him alive. Over time, his remains were incorporated into the mountain that rose over him.

Yet another ancient myth is often associated with the etymology of the peninsula's port. Local lore has it that Apollo, the Olympian god of the sun, verse, and music (amongst many others), was struck by the golden arrow of Eros (Cupid) as retaliation for having mocked the god of love. Immediately, Apollo was imbued with a deep lust for a Naiad Nymph named Daphne. Eros then drew a lead arrow and struck Daphne, instilling her with a seething hatred for Apollo. Daphne made clear her revulsion towards him, but the lovesick Apollo remained undeterred and continued to pursue her. In an effort to escape the harassment, Daphne fled to the port of Mount Athos and remained there for some time. The port of Mount Athos was then christened "Daphne," as it continues to be known today.

Edal Anton Lefterov's picture of Daphne

The blessed – or, as some would say, cursed – pinnacle of Mount Athos was also a setting frequently referenced by fabled wordsmiths in ancient Greece. Homer and Aeschylus, the "Father of Tragedy," described the summit as the former residence of Zeus and Apollo prior to their relocation to Mount Olympus. The peninsula's peak has also been credited with hastening victories of multiple battles. For one, a great bonfire ignited on the crest of the mountain supposedly served as a beacon that led to the capture of Troy.

Shortly after Zeus and Apollo moved to Mount Olympus, a total of five cities cropped up on the Athos peninsula, where they flourished until the 3rd century BCE. These communities coexisted in harmony for several centuries, fostering their own distinct customs and trading with and alongside one another with little friction. These were built on the summit and along the slopes, including Cleonae, Thyssus, and Acrothoon, the last of which was renowned for the ripe old ages of its residents. Colonies consisting of Pelasgians set up camp on the foot of the mountain.

Alas, the citizens of the peninsula were far too materialistic and thankless for the Olympian gods' liking, so to teach the ingrates a lesson, the vindictive deities shook the peninsula with an apocalyptic earthquake that decimated every last city. Those who survived decamped to the mainland, and Athos remained largely vacant until 368 BCE, when it fell under the jurisdiction of the Macedonian King Philip II, later succeeded by his son, Alexander the Great. According to the works of Plutarch and Strabo, Dinocrates, the chief architect and the ambitious mastermind behind the city of Alexandria, began to conceive a design that would outshine Alexandria. The plan was to carve Mount Athos into the likeness of Alexander, leading some modern historians to refer to the idea as the "classical Greek Mount Rushmore." An entire city would be nestled upon the colossal sculpture's outstretched palm. Draped over his right shoulder and arm were streams and cascading waterfalls that would be linked to the Aegean Sea.

Such a magnificent monument would seem almost impossible to turn down, yet that is precisely what Alexander did. "Let the mountain stand as it is," was Alexander's alleged response to Dinocrates. "It is sufficient that another king perpetuated his arrogance by having a canal cut through it."

An ancient bust of King Philip II of Macedon

An 18th century imagination of what the monument would look like

Andrew Dunn's picture of an ancient bust of Alexander

This "arrogant" king was none other than Xerxes, the Persian emperor from the 5th century BCE best known for invading Greece during the Second Persian War. During the First Persian War, the Persians had a fleet badly damaged when it barreled into Athos' cragged coastline. Hoping to prevent a repeat of such a tragedy, Xerxes dispatched a crew of men to the peninsula and ordered them to create a canal that sliced through the isthmus between the mainland and Athos a decade later. This allowed later fleets to sail through the shortcut safely, as opposed to having to tackle the dicey southern point, Cape Akrothoos of the Athos peninsula. With the help of the canal, Xerxes successfully invaded the Greek mainland, but after the Battle of Salamis and the Battle of Plataea, the Persians were ultimately driven out of Greek terrain.

Whether this canal truly existed is still a matter of dispute, with some claiming the canal was only partially built before Xerxes's architects were made to abandon the project, and others asserting the project was never even started. Believers today point the cynical to the supposed dregs and remnants of the canal in its purported location on the peninsula, which hints at the one-time existence of an artificial channel.

D. Bachman's picture of the peninsula from the summit of Mount Athos

The Rise of the Rock Pillars

"They pierce the clouds

of witnesses

to ancient work of holy part...

They tell stories centuries old

of feet too bold

to touch the earth..." - Lawrence Willson

The intrepid souls who scaled the 1,312 foot sandstone pillars, a striking departure from the plain of Thessaly, were not innovative intellectuals equipped with costly state-of-the-art tools and futuristic technology, nor were they adrenaline-seeking, able-bodied knights with a penchant for heights. Quite the opposite, the conquerors of these stone mountains were religious hermits who sought a more intimate relationship with the Lord, and later, they were humble Eastern Orthodox monks fleeing from the throes of invasion and persecution suffered at the hands of the Ottoman Turks. Heeding the impracticability of piecing together fortresses and bulwarks from resources and time that they could not afford, the ascetics embraced the heaven-made structures at their disposal and cunningly made them work to their advantage.

The activity at Meteora is documented, but how did this rock formation come about in the first place? The most popular theory is one propounded by 19th century German geologist, Alexander Philipson. Philipson, who inspected the sedimentary phenomenon in the latter half of the 1800s and proposed that a massive body of water once sat where the Meteora rocks now stand. This volume of water, now known as the Thessaly Sea, was formed via ice and rainwater about 60 million years ago, during the Paleogene Period. The seabed accumulated gravel, soil, and other matter as time progressed, carried over from the sloshing waters of the estuaries in the northern half of central Europe. 30 million years later, "deltaic cones" began to jut out of the gradually receding waterline of the Thessaly Sea.

It was around this time that Europe was rocked by a mighty and equally devastating earthquake. This quake, followed by centuries of rainfall, ice storms, and winter thaws that came with the cyclic seasons, gave rise to the central and southern portion of what is now the land of Europe. The shimmering stream of a Thessalian gorge now called the Vale of Tempe was supposedly filled during this time. When this overflowing Thessalian stream could no longer be contained, it burst forth into the crystalline Aegean Sea, and the stress produced the split of the "united mass" of deltaic cones nearby. The fences of sediment were shaved down by the water's movements until they were no more than moist, marshy flatlands.

The formation of the rocks at Meteora followed a similar pattern, best summed up in this passage provided by *Greek Landscapes*: "At the western edge of [the Thessaly Sea], near the Pindos Mountains, a number of streams formed a delta right where Meteora is today as they emptied their waters into the lake. Just imagine how much sedimentary rock and other materials were on the move when the huge volume of water was able to rush away from this region in a flash flood. The conglomerate was formed over thousands of years of stone, sand, and mud deposits at the edge of the lake, and when the lake dried, the softer sandstone around it eroded away, leaving Meteora standing."

The growing rocks were continuously broken apart and sculpted by corrosion over the millennia that followed. Fueled by more earthquakes, blustery winds, tempestuous rains, and their rubble-like bearings, more than 1,000 outcrops were created, protruding from the rising seabed. When the last pools of the Thessaly Sea had evaporated, there remained, as 19th century British diplomat, traveler, and author Robert Curzon, put it, "a series of...tall, thin, smooth, needle-like rocks." These rocks were held together by the "dissolution of...limestone rocks and the pressure they received." According to *Experiment* magazine, the present structure and layout of the Meteora rocks has remained relatively unchanged for over 3,000-4,000 years.

Religious connotations attached to the Meteoran rocks, as proven by the etiological narratives spun by the locals, is nothing new. Ignorant of the fundamentals of geology, the first residents of the surrounding plains propagated myths that they believed satisfactorily decoded the creation of these stone pillars. Some claimed that a rain of rocks befell this region not long after the Great Deluge, and that this gravelly shower was prompted by an unnamed Olympian god who either desired to erect a border of sorts between his earthly kingdoms, or simply decided to add some color and texture to the verdant flatlands. Others pointed to the Titanomachy, or the infamous Battle of the Titans, a long war fought between the 12 Olympian gods and their predecessors, the Titans of Mount Othrys. Amidst the exchange of flashing fire bolts, whirling tides of water, and ground-fracturing quakes, Zeus ordered the Hecatonchires – a trio of giants with hundreds of hands – to uproot enormous boulders from the ground and hurl them at the Titans. The projectiles that missed the dodging Titans either crashed into the Aegean or fell upon the land that would become Meteora with such force that it pierced deep into the earth. They were unmovable by even the fiercest and shrillest gales, but some of the boulders collided and splintered, creating the more slender pillars seen today. In the end, the younger Olympians emerged triumphant.

Others asserted that Meteora's rocks were because a game that went awry. The rough, but friendly contact sport, some say, required the Olympian gods to toss about massive rocks, but a few gods overthrew some rocks so much that they soared past the heads of their teammates, landing in and penetrating the Meteoran grasslands. Others say the formations were pushed upward by the hefty bodies of players sliding across the flatlands, with the sand mounds created by the impact later solidifying into stone. Another myth had the Greek gods molding these pillars from sand and earth with their fingers in some kind of contest.

In later centuries, particularly during medieval times, locals began to ascribe the "planting" of the rocks to their exceptionally advanced ancestors, whose communities flourished over 5,000 years ago. Since they lived in an age prior to written, tangible records, current knowledge regarding these prehistoric Greeks is a blend of lore and educated guesses.

Centuries before the foundation of the classical city states and the introduction of Athenian democracy, Greece was tamed by the Pelasgians and the Minyans. The Minyans, who occupied what would one day become Thessaly, most likely emerged during the Bronze Age, circa 2600 BCE. Though exact details about their life are scarce, historians have determined that they resided in the ancient city of Almonia in Thessaly, ruled by a monarch they called "King Minyas." The Minyans, as maintained by local legends, were an extremely advanced people, and their technological and architectural savvy was reflected in the fantastic monuments they supposedly left behind. The Minyans have been credited with producing labyrinthine tunnels that linked one city to the other, resilient fortresses, and other tremendous structures that "defy all logic." That they did this without blueprints, or even a written language, makes their contributions all the more astounding.

The incredible nature of the Minyans' handiwork was perhaps why some remain adamant that they had extra help. Some theorize that they collaborated with a neighboring civilization that has since been buried under the sands of time, whereas others remain convinced that they received supernatural assistance, whether from extraterrestrials or a troop of giants and the Cyclopes, a "wild race" of hulking and crude-mannered one-eyed creatures. This was the only way, some reasoned, that the Minyans were able to lift enormous rocks, boulders, and other weighty building materials in a time before cranes and pulley systems.

Some examples their feats are the roughly-built, but grand Mycenaean walls, otherwise known as the "Cyclopean Walls." These were pieced together by slabs of limestone and held together by crushed limestone gravel, an accomplishment that's even more remarkable by the fact that it was impossible for a pair of mules to move even a single block of these "unwrought stones."

Given that background, it's no wonder that people also came up with various theories about Meteora's origins. Some attribute Meteora's origins to the Minyans alone, believing that the environment cultivated by King Minyas was enough to engender this unbelievable feat. King Minyas was depicted by chroniclers as a prudent and peace-loving sovereign who prized progress, which he insisted could only be attained through knowledge and the broadening of horizons. As a matter of fact, Minyas was one of the first rulers to develop a government-funded educational system for his subjects. His focus on education apparently led to generations upon generations of liberal-minded explorers, ingenious architects, and inventive artists.

To put into better perspective the unparalleled skills of the Minyan builders, their magnum opus was a once-glittering citadel named "Gla" of Orchomenos. On top of Gla's mighty, two-mile-long Cyclopean walls, the architects succeeded in the astonishing task of draining the lake surrounding the petite island so as to create a more stable foundation for the citadel. Nobody's sure how they drained the lake, but with this logic in mind, some argue that the Minyans most likely emptied what was left of the Thessaly Sea as well. People still debate whether or not it was intentional, or whether it even happened, but according to this theory, the draining of that lake led to the formation of the Meteoran rocks.

The First People of Meteora

"Don't explain your philosophy – embody it through doing the work that matters, work that lasts." – Epictetus, a 1st century CE Greek philosopher

The robustly-built catacombs and tunnels underneath the Byzantine Church of Virgin Mary in Kalabaka (also written as "Kalambaka"), the city built at the foot of Meteora, is another architectural venture attributed to the Minyans. Locals today claim that the tunnels connected Kalabaka to Trikka (now the city of Trikala in Thessaly) in their heyday, a full 12.5 miles away from Meteora. The proto-Greek people of Trikka were first referenced in *The Iliad*, attributed to the legendary poet Homer, in the 8th century BCE: "From Trikka, and Ithome of the crags, from

Oechalia home of Eurytus, came thirty hollow ships, commanded by Asclepius' two sons, the skillful healers Podaleirius and Machaon."

Trikka and the aforementioned ancient cities were not the only metropolises cited in *The Iliad*, because the locals near Meteroa also made quite a number of significant appearances. Nearby residents who lived by the base of the rock pillars in the city of Eginion (now Kalabaka) were said to have been among those aboard the 30 war vessels captained by medically-trained generals Machaon and his brother, Podaleirius. The Meteoran soldiers were, alongside the seafaring warriors, battling the Trojans of Troy on behalf of the Achaeans, or the Greeks. The war, now known as the infamous "Trojan War," was triggered by the kidnapping of Helen, wife of Spartan King Menelaus.

The citizens of Eginion are said to have been just as, if not more pious than the future residents of Meteora, but they bowed before a different deity, or in this case, a selection of deities. There is evidence that the structure that preceded the Byzantine Church of Virgin Mary was a handsome temple erected by the Eginions and devoted to Apollo, the Greek god of music, healing, and truth and prophecy. While they were not as technologically advanced as the fabled Pelasgians and Minyans, they constructed a nice city, complete with a unique, well-rounded, and enduring culture. The Eginion locals also flourished and benefited from the burst of creativity that took place in Greece from 500-300 BCE, and their economy was durable enough to sustain itself for centuries, even minting and utilizing their own coins. Not much about the local currency is known today, but they probably resembled the coins used in neighboring cities, consisting of round, flat discs of silver or bronze stamped with the silhouettes of native animals or the silhouette of a local ruler.

Moreover, while the Eginions weren't exactly the most progressive when compared to the more prominent Greek cities during the time, they were competent enough to subjugate and coexist with the wild animals and harsh weather conditions in the area. The northern and eastern parts of the region were subjected to cyclical, but abrupt weather patterns. During the summer months, humans and animals hid out in their huts and burrows to escape the dry, scorching heat, which averaged 90° Fahrenheit. Turbulent storms, which pestered the region year-round, doubled during the autumn months, serving as a gloomy prelude to bitterly cold, snow-laden winters.

The thick, almost jungle-like forests that sprouted from the fertile remnants of the dried seabed provided more than ample shelter, shade, food, and resources for a wide range of mammals. Close to what is now Mantania Village is the Kalogriani Forest, home to a diverse collection of elm, sycamore, dogwood, oak, and fir trees. Animals and insects came in varying sizes, from common gray wolves and brown bears to an assortment of rabbits. The Chrisomilia Forest, situated next to its town and namesake, was populated by wolves, foxes, and bears that were attracted to the woodland's maple, fir, and oak trees.

From the very beginning, Meteora's forests also served as a sanctuary for multiple species of fowl, including four types of vultures, songbirds (thrush), partridges, "alpine swift...crag martin[s]...red-rumped swallow[s]...and...birds of prey...[such as] honey buzzard[s]...black kites...short-toed eagle[s]...Levant sparrowhawk[s]...peregrine falcon[s]...black stork[s]," and European rollers.

Outside of the largely fictitious events woven together by Homer, the real Eginions were reportedly a proud and patriotic people who did not hesitate to give their lives to defend their territories, or for the Achaean cause. The locals also provided aid to numerous Greek military campaigns, including the donation of domesticated stallions to the Thessalian cavalry who charged alongside Alexander the Great. This excerpt, included in Meteora's official travel website and *Ancient Greece Reloaded*, elaborates on the Eginions' reverence for the Macedonian monarch: "And under the command of Alexander, they fought and died on the numerous battlegrounds, fighting to subdue the great Persian Empire, [as well as in the Battles of] Granicus, Issus, and Gaugamela. These proud Thessalians stood alongside their great King all the way to the high mountains of Hindu-Kish, witnessing the edges of the then-known world and reaching the doorsteps of [the] Himalaya[s]. Many years later, the people of Meteora saw the countless Roman legions marching with their generals and passing through [the] Pindos Mountains' narrow passes on their way to either Italy, or to the East..."

Andrew Dunn's picture of an ancient bust of Alexander the Great

For thousands of years, Eginions conducted rituals, particularly during the lunar months, which involved the preparation of animal sacrifices, special cakes, and blessed war booty. They also participated in traditional games, such as the Olympics, to pray for good fortune and to show their gratitude in the event of a victory. However, the sweeping introduction of Christianity to Greece, beginning with Saint Paul's missionary work in 49 CE, ushered the region and the Eginions into a whole new era. Old temples that stood for centuries were razed to the ground and replaced with wide, domed Orthodox Christian churches topped with distinctive clover-armed crosses. The town itself was christened with a new name, and henceforth, Eginion was to be known as "Stagoi."

The Eginions and their descendants assisted the first hermits, recluses, and dissidents to establish their man-sized crevices within and atop the rock pillars, with some even helping to construct their unconventional dwellings. The residents of Stagoi and their heirs, in turn, assisted the monks that eventually came in raising their monasteries and communities, serving as a great source of neighborly aid in the centuries that followed. And it was they who granted shelter, food, and comfort to the Byzantine emperors, princes, and nobles that came to seek blessings from the Meteoran monks.

Solitary Christian hermits and pagan loners bearing no ties to brotherhoods have undoubtedly taken up residence in the crannies of Meteora's rocks since the 1st century CE, and while the place is now renowned for the "suspended" monasteries built by 14th century Eastern Orthodox monks, geological data shows that they were predated by another monastic community, one that found refuge in these parts in the 10th century CE.

The very first monasteries in Western Europe, believed to have been established by followers of Saint Benedict of Nursia in Italy during the early years of the 6th century CE, were formed as a way to isolate the most devout from the persecutions of the heretical and oppressive Roman authorities at the time. Furthermore, the rigid lifestyle, shaped by constant prayer, rigorous discipline, and celibacy, was a new way to express utmost dedication to the "one true Lord." It was, in their view, far more honorable to detach themselves from the chaotic political climate and become self-reliant so as to allow themselves to pledge their lives entirely to God.

Some say the first monks – Varnavas (Barnabas), Nilos, and Andronikos – were driven to the extremes of Meteora's rocks for political reasons. About a century prior to the beginning of what is now remembered as the "Great Schism" (the divorce between the Roman Catholic Church and the Eastern Orthodox Church), the two factions that had arisen within the Christian Church had become more defined than ever. Clues of an impending split first emerged in the middle of the 1st millennium CE, cemented by the Council of Chalcedon in 451, which saw the opposing sides aggressively dissecting the true nature of Christ, and the rift between the factions only continued to expand in the following centuries. By the early 900s, the relationship between the two branches of Christianity seemed unsalvageable, for they could not find middle ground regarding their clashing views.

The role of the Roman Catholic Pope was a particularly pressing topic. Though the Orthodox Christians acknowledged the presence of the Latin ecclesiastical patriarch, they disapproved of the superiority that came with his position. The pope, the Orthodox Christians argued, was just as fallible as the rest of his religious subjects, and was not vested with any supplementary powers simply because of his title. The animosity between both factions grew even more inflamed with the seemingly endless debate about the sanctity behind icon veneration, which pitted the Iconodules (those for the practice) against the Iconoclasts. Conflicting values regarding the conduct and lifestyles of their clergymen also drove the opposing sects further apart. For example, the Catholics specified that their priests be wholly abstinent from sex, refrain from overindulgence in alcohol, and other moral codes. While the Orthodox Christian priests were required to be upstanding moral pillars of society, they were allowed to take a wife.

Some say Varnavas and the monks that followed were chased away by the internal turmoil and administrative conflicts that threatened to tear apart the local Orthodox Church during these trying times. Other historians, however, claim the motivations behind the building of the 10th century Meteoran monasteries were far more optimistic. The monastic community installed by Varnavas was not founded as a way to permanently quarantine themselves from the toxicities within the Orthodox sect, but rather as a way to celebrate their devotion.

In the year 963, Byzantine Emperor Nicephorus II Phocas pledged to place the Orthodox *lavra* (monastery) erected by Saint Athanasius on Mount Athos under imperial protection, and it continues to be the heart of the monastic republic today. Around the same time, Saint Symeon, a Galatia native, abbot of Constantinople's St. Mamas Monastery, and one of the Orthodox Church's three "Theologians," published a guide of sorts pertaining to the monk's "mystical" routines and prayers. Symeon's system functioned as a model for Orthodox monasteries across Greece, and helped to shape and accelerate the evolution of the faith's spirituality.

With Orthodox Christianity now being more firmly established, a small, ambitious group of monks set out to a different corner of Greece to establish monastic and religious centers that would allow them to carry out their distinct customs without intervention from the authorities of the rival sect. The wandering eye of a roaming monk by the name of Varnavas settled upon the peculiar rock pillars in Stagoi. Thus, between 950 and 960 (or, according to some sources, 980), Varnavas shimmied up the surrounding mass of boulders on the northern part of the rock complex, stopping at an uninhabited cave on the side of one of the porous pillars. This wide, but low-roofed cavity was, thanks to Varnvas's blood, sweat, and tears, converted into a chapel he called the Chapel of the Aghio Pnevma (Holy Spirit).

Majesty was the furthest thing from Varnavas' mind. To the untrained eye from below, above, afar, or even up close, the unadorned chapel entrance looked no different from the shadowy hollows peppered throughout the facades of the rock formations. As that suggests, this was to be an unobtrusive place of worship that focused on the power of prayer, rather than needless ostentation. One would find no more than a short stone altar with a cross and either a portrait of a martyred saint or a relic as its centerpiece; the only traces of color were the candles Varnavas dutifully lit, along with a light bundle of freshly-picked flowers. This millennium-old chapel still exists today, tucked away in the mossy corner of what is now known as the "Aghio Pnevma Rock," or the "Rock of the Holy Spirit," and is identifiable by a narrow, teal-blue door.

The Skete of the Holy Spirit was raised shortly thereafter. The skete was occupied by a handful of monks who accompanied Varnavas, most likely those who helped construct the chapel. In contrast to cenobitic complexes, which had monks sharing lodgings and fulfilling their assigned duties as a single unit, the monks are believed to have lived a more idiorrhythmic lifestyle. Varnavas and his companions lived in separate huts or cells, and they were expected to more or less sustain themselves, but they convened on a daily basis to worship as one.

Little can be confirmed about the 10th century monks of Meteora, but a local legend about a monk named Nilos continues to be circulated to this day. Based on this story, when Nilos, one of the older monks, was on the verge of death, he divulged to his fellow monks his final wishes. Instead of being cloaked in a square of ceremonial cloth and having his corpse carried down to Stagoi for a traditional burial, he requested permission to drift through the Meteoran forests upon his dying breaths, so that he could become supper for the wild animals that lived there. However, the *protas*, or abbot of the monastic community, learned about Nilos's plans. Criticizing the abnormality of the practice, or perhaps fretting over the animals being given a taste of human flesh (which might lead to unprompted animal attacks), the *protas* rejected Nilos's request. Upon his death, they ordered Nilos to be put to eternal rest the Orthodox Christian way.

Word soon trickled out of Stagoi and spread across nearby cities, perking the ears of more nature-loving, soul-searching monks. In the early years of the 11th century CE, a monk named Andronikos from Crete founded the Cloister of the Transfiguration of Jesus. Little information about this cloister has survived, but this elevated open-air arcade was presumably attached to a small chapel of the same name. The villagers who lived below these fledgling monastic communities were inspired by the sacred, austere lives led by those in the caves of the "heavenly columns," and a few even expressed their wishes to join the cause. The Skete of Stagoi, otherwise known as the "Skete of Doupiani," was set up at the foot of these pillars, a 10 year project that began in 1150.

The Skete of Stagoi is now considered the "first ascetic state" in Meteora, as well as the first full-fledged idiorrhythmic monastic community. They were the first in the region to list and adhere to an official set of rules and code of conduct, and to be governed by an executive board of elder brothers, headed by a local monk named Nilos. With the help of the villagers, Nilos and the monks fashioned together a modest, sturdy church next to the Pyxari Rock, right below what would become the Monastery of St. Nicholas Anapafsas. It was dedicated to and dubbed the "*Panaghia Doupiani*," or the Church of the Virgin Mary of Doupiani. The valley adjacent to these rocks, now known as the "Valley of Panaghia," is sandwiched between the Pyxari and Amparia Rocks.

A picture of the town of Kalabaka from Meteora

The establishment of the church drew even more solitary souls to the skete. Throughout the week, the monks kept to themselves in their designated cave dwellings, with their lives quite literally revolving around routine prayer and sleep. They only exited their caves on Sundays to attend the weekly service held at the Church of the Virgin Mary.

As time progressed, the simple and serene culture of piety maintained by the Meteoran monks became more and more appealing to Orthodox Christians who either felt out of place amidst the increasing corruptions of city life or were emboldened by the Great Schism. Some joined the existing communities, while others founded monastic societies of their own, assembling their own private chapels and hermitages within or next to the Meteoran caves, which were called "*proseuchadia.*" The growing presence of Orthodox monks, who began to appear around the Rocks of Doupiani, the Holy Spirit, and Sourloti, only reinforced Meteora's reputation as a hallowed place.

Alas, while the better part of the residents of Stagoi and nearby villages applauded the abstention of the Meteoran monks and commended their devotion to godliness, they unwittingly became the targets of the greedy and the desperate. Increasing rumors about the real motivations behind the founding of these churches and *proseuchadia* only further whetted their appetites. The monks, as purported by these rumors, had been tasked with guarding monstrous mounds of gleaming gold, jewels, and treasures owned by the Byzantine emperors and nobles, which explained all the secrecy and the remoteness of these cave-chapels. As such, the chapels and sketes were subject to a string of thefts, and though most were thwarted, a few thieves managed to escape with at least a few precious relics. The harassment became so relentless that the monks on lower ground abandoned their caves, choosing to relocate to higher levels.

Another notable Meteoran community that was founded during the early 12th century was the Skete of Theotokos, centered around the Chapel of the Dormition of Theotokos (Chapel of the Assumption of the Virgin Mary). Also known as the *"Protato"* or the *"Kyriako,"* it is situated on the southern part of the Doupiani pillar, upon the ruins of a dilapidated Christian basilica, and operated by the *protas* of the Skete of Stagoi. The chapel became a kind of nerve center for the Meteoran hermitages - apart from hosting weekly services for the monks of its primary skete, the chapel also acted as conference hall for regular meetings held by the skete heads of Meteora, wherein they aired, reviewed, and found solutions to their grievances as a team.

The Byzantine Era

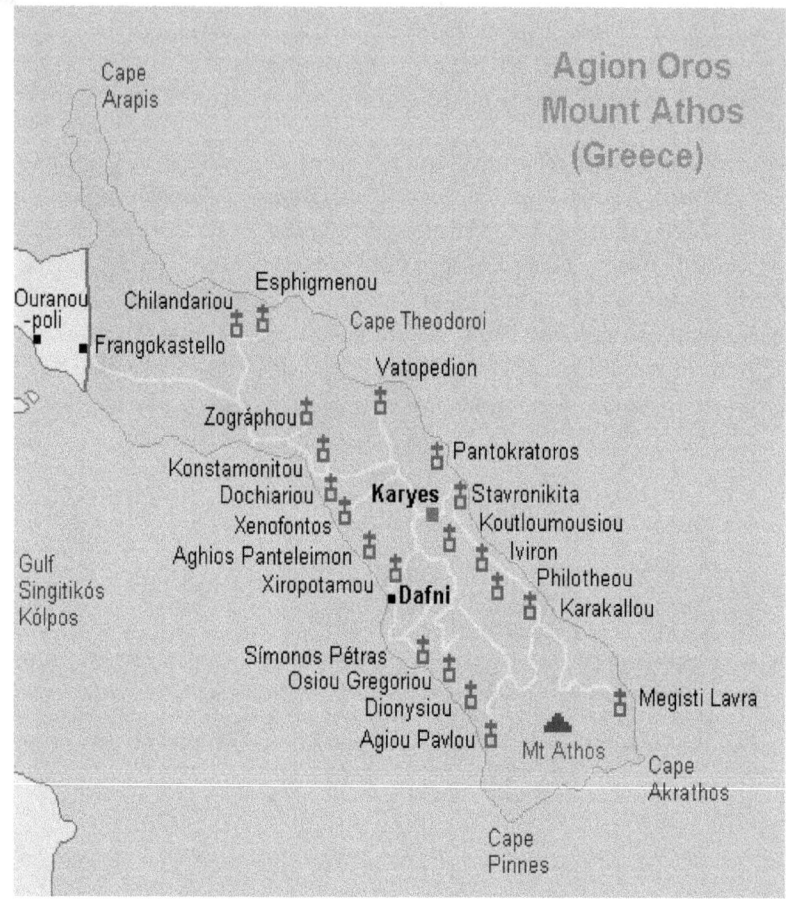

A map of various monasteries on the peninsula

"It is impossible to save one's soul without devotion to Mary and without her protection." – attributed to Anselm of Canterbury

Naturally, the Christian chapter of Mount Athos' history unfolded only after the beginning of the Common Era, and ironically, the ostensibly anti-woman culture within Athos, as maintained by its present locals, was conceived by a woman. According to the locals, that woman was none other than the mother of Jesus.

According to this account, in the summer of 49, Mary was invited to Cyprus by a post-resurrected Lazarus. To this, she readily agreed and boarded a small boat, but as fate would have it, a dreadful storm struck, steering the helpless vessel to the eastern coast of the Athonite peninsula, close to the present monastery of Iveron. The disoriented, but otherwise unhurt Mary staggered out of the broken boat. As soon as she took in the beauty of her surroundings, the soles of her feet sinking into the toasty sand, all panic and fear melted away. "This mountain is holy ground," she proclaimed to her son, her eyes fixed upon the mist cloaked over the Athonite peak. "Let it now be my portion. Here let me remain for eternity."

What happened next was nothing short of a miracle, one that could only be powered by the heavens. Once Mary started towards the slopes, the splendid temple devoted to Apollo, built on the Athonite summit, crumbled. This triggered a domino effect, and one by one, sculptures of pagan statues and other "false idols" either toppled over or disintegrated. Left standing amidst the rubble was the stone statue of Apollo on the peak of the mountain, which came to life and thundered across the peninsula: "Heed my words – I am a false idol. You must renounce me and come forth to pay tribute to the *Panaghia*, the true mother of God." With that, Apollo self-destructed.

Hermits and villagers alike did as they were ordered and came forth to honor their new matriarch. Each was baptized, cleansed of their pagan sins, and thenceforth tasked with carrying the Christian torch.

Author Gregory Palamas transcribed Mary's promissory speech to her new subjects in the *Life of St. Peter the Athonite*: "In Europe, there is a mountain, very high and very beautiful, which extends towards the south and very deeply into the sea. This is the mountain that I have chosen out of all the earth, and I have decided to make of it the country of the monastic order. I have consecrated it to be henceforth my dwelling: this is why people will call it the 'Holy Mountain.' All who shall come to live there after having decided to fight the battle against the common enemy of the human race will find me at their side throughout their lives…I will be their invincible aid, I will teach them what they must do, and what they must avoid. I myself shall be their tutor, their physician, their nurse. I shall take care to give them both food and the care that their bodies require, and that which is necessary for their souls, to inspire and invigorate them, so they depart not from virtue. And all who finish their lives on this mountain in a spirit of love for God and repentance, I promise to recommend to my Son and God that He accord them complete remission of their sins."

Despite Mary's alleged arrival in the 1st century CE, Orthodox Christianity did not enter the Athonite mainstream until the advent of the Byzantine Empire. It was only during the Council of Nicaea in 325 CE that this brand of Christianity was declared the official religion, and governmental headquarters were transferred to Byzantium, which would soon become Constantinople 5 years later. The Western Roman Empire collapsed in 476 CE, but its Eastern, predominantly Hellenistic counterpart in the Mediterranean – the Byzantine Empire – endured for almost another 1,000 years.

As determined by the Council of Chalcedon in 451 CE, the Christian world of the 5th century was split into five patriarchates, which were as follows: Rome, spearheaded by the pope as its patriarch; Antioch; Alexandria; Jerusalem; and Constantinople. Byzantine Emperor Flavius Marcian was appointed head of church and state for Constantinople, and Marcian's successors continued to reap the rewards of this title well into the 7th century, remaining the patriarch of the Eastern Orthodox Church even after the Muslim Saracens' capture of Antioch, Alexandria, and Jerusalem.

Riveting legends aside, knowledge of Athonite residents between prehistoric times and the 9th century CE is flimsy at best, if only because archaeologists are prohibited from digging or "desecrating" the hallowed land. Some historians believe that the first hermits in Athos were asylum seekers who fled during the Arab incursions into Byzantine territory, while others insist they were Iconodules (those who supported the controversial veneration of religious icons) shunned by Iconoclast emperors. Furthermore, there are the Virgin-deniers who insist that the natives were nonconforming recluses from nearby lands who were simply drawn to the unparalleled, and therefore magnetic solitude that Athos had to offer. Christian monks – some disgruntled by internal ecclesiastical corruptions and others simply looking for deeper spiritual fulfillment – eventually chanced upon the peninsula in the 4th century CE and took to the mountains to erect their new homes. At this stage, the Athonite monks lived hermetically, for the concept of communal monastic societies had only just been inaugurated in the Egyptian desert around this time. The tradition gradually spread across the Middle East before penetrating Europe sometime around the late 7th century or early 8th century.

By the year 843, according to the local 10th century historian Genesios, there was already a primitive, but well-established monastic community on Mount Athos. The community was composed mainly of a sizable group of monks who arrived in the early 700s and were present at the Seventh Ecumenical Council of Nicaea (also referred to as the Second Council of Nicaea) in 787. The conference revolved around the controversial issue of the era: icons and their place in Christian worship. This feud between the Iconodules and the Iconoclasts first arose in 726, when Emperor Leo III demanded the removal of Christ's portrait above Constantinople's Chalke Gate.

On the one hand, Iconoclasts were adamant that icon veneration defied Scripture, and some zealous Iconoclasts took such offense to the practice that they would sneak into private homes and churches to deface and dismantle these false idols in the name of God. As for the Iconodules, or Iconophiles, their counterargument is summed up by an excerpt provided by *Khan Academy*: "Images of Christ do not depict natures, being either divine or human, but a concrete person – Jesus Christ." They, did, however, concur when it came to outlawing depictions of God the Father: "God prohibited any representation of God (or anything that could be worshiped as a god) because it was impossible to depict the invisible God."

The discourse was heated, but in the end, the council ruled in favor of the Iconodules. The practice was to be restored, and artworks devoted to Christ and other saintly figures were proclaimed "open books to remind [one] of God." As stated by the verdict, "Icons...are to be kept in churches and honored with the same relative veneration as is shown to other material symbols, such as the 'precious and life-giving Cross' and the Book of the Gospels." 22 canons were simultaneously published. Canon 7 affirmed the necessary installation of relics in all churches, Canon 18 banned all women from lodging in monasteries and the houses of bishops, and Canon 20 forbade the establishment of "double" or co-ed monasteries.

Over time, the solitude the Athonite monks so prized was interrupted time and time again, both inadvertently and deliberately by external forces who yearned to claim the slice of paradise for themselves. The Battle of Thasos, fought in October of 829, concluded with the Cretan Arabs' triumph over the Byzantines. As reported by the *Theophanes Continuatus*, the official collection of annals commissioned by Emperor Constantine VII, the Byzantine navy was crushed, losing almost all of their warships. Thus, the Mediterranean, Mount Athos included, entered its first major dark age, and in the decades that followed, vulnerable Byzantine islands were subjected to a string of vicious raids carried out by Saracen generals and rogue pirates. With supplementary help from Byzantine Islam converts, the Saracens succeeded in seizing, destroying, and looting the Cyclades before directing their attention towards Mount Athos. The brutality of the ambushes that targeted the pitifully protected peninsula rendered it abandoned for a few decades.

This state of desertion ended in 860 with the arrival of Friar Efthymios the Younger, which coincided with the rise of Macedonian Emperor Basil I. The debris was cleared, the burned patches punctuating the land were replenished, and a small number of huts, known as the "Skiti of Saint Basil," were constructed around Efthymios' home by the *Krya Nera*, or the "Dark Spring," that trickled down from the mountain. With the blessings of the pious emperor, the retired Archbishop of Crete, Basil the Confessor, installed a modest monastery where the harbor of the Hilandar Monastery now stands.

The Hilandar Monastery in the 1890s

Much like the traumatized monks who were forced to vacate the peninsula during the Saracen raids, Emperor Basil was shattered by the mutilation of the Holy Mountain, and he was resolved to squash such a recurrence. In 883, Basil formally took the peninsula under his imperial wing when he issued a "gold-sealed" *sigillion* that banned all shepherds from grazing on the peninsula and inhibited all other potential intruders from entry. Not even state officials were allowed to set foot on Athos without permission. Two years later, Basil emancipated the Athonite monks from the dominion of the episcopal see in Hierissus, cementing the Athonites' authority over the *Agion Oros*.

The cenobitic lifestyle, which centered on communal living – namely, a society wherein everyone was assigned their own roles and expected to contribute equally – was most likely employed far earlier, but it only caught on amongst the Athonite monasteries in the mid-10th century. Interestingly, reception of this practice was initially split down the middle. There were those who championed the organization of monastic life, and formed monasteries in neighboring territories accordingly. On the opposite end of the spectrum were the anti-cenobites, who condemned the cenobites' rigid liturgical system, which fused the "solemn Liturgy of the Hours" with the practice of hourly prayer. They were instead proponents of more "moderate" nine-ode "structured canons," or "hymnography," which were segregated into different anthologies and chanted throughout scheduled liturgical cycles. Famous anti-cenobite St. Blasios of Amorion endeavored to usher in the more relaxed studite practice in the year 900, to no avail.

Following the death of Emperor Basil I in 908, the peninsula's residents found themselves paddling through gray waters yet again. The Athonites had to act swiftly, for rival monks from St. Colobos, near Hierissus, were once again flexing their jaws for the coveted Mount Athos. Fortunately, they managed to secure the protection of Basil's successor, Leo VI, and remained more or less an independent entity. 34 years later, Emperor Romanos I Lecapenos strengthened the imperial protection over Athos by extending an annual pension of one gold nugget each to the Athonite monks. Technically speaking, the monks were now "salaried public servants," so they were expected to pray for and bless the sovereign, his empire, and all their military campaigns.

By the 950s, the Athonites had already developed a functioning governing system, and even a set of legislation of their own. Seated within the uppermost level of the pyramid was the *Protos* (Premier), the governor of all Athonite monastic communities. The *protos* was charged with the representation of the peninsula in domestic and international affairs, and vested with a slew of managerial powers, such as the appointment and dismissal of abbots. Up until 1312, the *protos* was named by the emperor. All *protos* after the fact were elected by members of the *Iera Epistasia,* or "Holy Administration." This board of monastic executives, in turn, oversaw the *Iera Koinotita,* or "Holy Community," which comprised delegates from each of the peninsula's monasteries.

More titles were added to the *Protaton* in Karyes, the administrative capital of Athos, between the latter half of the 10th and the early 11th centuries. Such posts include the *oikonomos* (household-manager), the *ecclesiarchis* (sacristans), and the *epitiritis* (procurator). The governing body convened in Karyes on three occasions each year – Christmas, Easter, and the Feast of the Koimesis of the Virgin on August 15th) – in conferences called *"synaxes"* to dissect the most pressing and contentious issues.

The arrival of Saint Athanasios the Athonite in 957 marked the dawn of another new age on the peninsula. Accompanying Athanasios, a former teacher from Constantinople, was future Emperor Nikephoros II, at the time a general. Together, the fierce duo succeeded in staving off multiple Saracen invasions. Five years later, Athanasios directed the refurbishment of the main church in Karyes. Following Nikephoros' ascension to the imperial throne in 963, secured through his politically motivated betrothal to Empress Theophano, he conquered Candia and regained Crete later that year. Profits from his conquest of Candia were used to fund what was known as the "Great Lavra" in the fall of 963. The Great Lavra was the concentration of the existing "scattered" monasteries into one monastic community, an institution that would reign superior within the Athonite community. During the imperial reign of Nikephoros, the lavra began to deviate from its humble beginnings. As Nicholaos Economidis of *Elpenor* put it, the lavra "was transformed into a lavishly endowed royal foundation for approximately 80 monks, with annual revenues in cash and kind and with lands and property exempt from taxation."

An icon of St. Athanasios

The Great Lavra, the grandest *koinobion* ("common life") monastery constructed by the Byzantine Empire thus far, boasted such innovative designs and methodical structure that its model was replicated by numerous monasteries within and outside of Mount Athos. Bearing this in mind, the Great Lavra was pioneering in more ways than one, for it was the first monastery to be granted independence from the Patriarch of Constantinople, along with the right to name its own bishop. These important new liberties were outlined in the three chrysobulls issued by

Nikephoros in 964. On top of their newfound independence, the lavra was formally guaranteed a pension of 244 gold pieces each year, as well as a substantial consignment of wheat.

A medieval depiction of Nikephoros

Athanasios personally superintended the compound's construction, which, upon its unveiling, featured the Basilica of the Theotokos, as well as individual cells, fountains, a refectory, hostel, kitchen, and a number of other amenities. The population of the complex only continued to rise over the years, escalating to 120 in less than a decade; halfway into the 11th century, that number soared to 700.

Seated close to the southeastern tongue of the peninsula, the Great Lavra, otherwise known as the "Monastery of Megisti Lavra," remains the oldest and grandest of all the Athonite monasteries. For a complex nearly 1,500 years old, the lavra remains in near pristine condition, save for the natural wear and tear prompted by the salty air. To the untrained eye, the enclosure seems more like a tiny, compact town, with a 15-tower fortress that guarded the complex and the treasures inside its 37 chapels and massive library, which housed over 30,000 printed books, 2,046 manuscripts, and 165 original codices. Also included in the lavra's spectacular relic collection were the *sakkos* and crown of Emperor Nikephoros, as well as the body of Athonasias himself, buried in the Chapel of Forty Martyrs.

Mates Il's picture of the Great Lavra

The *katholikon* of the monastery

The *katholikon*, or central church of the Great Lavra also served as the archetype of all future *katholika* erected on Mount Athos. Consecrated to the Annunciation of the Blessed Virgin Mary, the four-columned, cross-shaped structure consisted of only two stories, and was topped by a ribbed, hemispherical dome garnished with wavy edges. The first Athonite *Phiale*, a studded libation bowl constantly filled with holy water, was installed by the main entrance of the *katholikon*. In the 1400s, the Grand Lavra was reconsecrated, this time dedicated to a post-canonized Athanasios. The Lavra underwent routine renovations the following century, with the most significant addition being the colorful frescoes of biblical scenes and detailed portrait medallions of saints painted onto the walkway and the arched roof of the refectory in 1535. This was the work of Cretan painter and monk Theophanes Strelitsa, whose glowing portfolio included artwork found in the Meteora monasteries. The decision to coat the entire facade with red paint was made at a later date.

A fresco at Mount Athos depicting Saint Mercurius and Artemius of Antioch

Athanasios's pride in perfecting the Athonite way of life is reflected in the *Typikon*, a book listing the rubric for the religious services in 973, the year he authored it. "I have found by experience that it is right and beneficial...for all the brothers to live in common. All together they are to look to the same goal of salvation...They form one heart in their common life, one will, one desire, and one body, as the apostle prescribes."

As previously mentioned, the majority of the hermits openly resisted the intervention, as mankind tends to be when confronted with change. The studites resented the severity of the new worshiping customs, which included forced punctuality and maintaining absolute silence throughout these droning divine services. Others criticized the uncharacteristic extravagance of the compound, complete with bustling workshops, for it contradicted the very essence of the material-free solitude attached to conventional hermeticism.

Evidently, all protests were made in vain, for Nikephoros's successor, Emperor John I Tzimiskes, ultimately put the ball in the cenobites' court. In 972, the Great Lavra was issued its first official charter, called the "*Tragos*," which legitimized a regime that centered on the "coexistence of both traditional eremitic monasticism and the new cenobite system." The same charter also created the post of the *hegumens*, "spiritual fathers" or chief confessors of the different monastic communities, and rolled out a new set of rules all Athonite monks were to abide by.

Economidis explored some of these said rules in the following passage: "Solitary reclusion [sic] was permitted only to experienced monks, who were in addition required to observe a certain discipline...peregrination was not permitted. The *Tragos* further defined...the economic and social relations between hermits and monks, and monks and lay folk. Compulsory unpaid labor was abolished, and discipline was imposed on relations between monks: any who were quarrelsome were liable to be expelled." Furthermore, "the numbers of cattle owned by the foundations was severely restricted: only the Great Lavra...was permitted to own a yoke of oxen (for the purpose of kneading...bread)."

By the time the 10th century drew to a close, the bulk of the most prominent Athonite monasteries – including the Hilander, Vatopedi, Iveron, and Panteleimon, amongst others – had been established. There were a total of 46 monasteries on the peninsula (one source claims there was as many as 3,000).

The 10th century was also underscored by the active adoption of a law that would lead to what is arguably the most salient and delicate of the peninsula's present controversies. Included in the 10th century *Tragos* was a canon that called for the expulsion of all female animals on Mount Athos. Female cows, goats, dogs, ewes, and every other native mammal were banished from Athonite grounds, so as to never "defile [the eyes of the monks] with anything female." Only insects, birds, and cats (favored for their rodent-ridding abilities) were exempt from this rule. Needless to say, while it wasn't specified in this particular charter, it was second nature for women to avoid the peninsula. It wasn't until 1046 that Canon 18, issued by the Second Council of Nicaea in 787, was reiterated in the chrysobull of Emperor Constantine Monomachos. Monomachos' bull also ordered all eunuchs and young boys to avoid Athos, for their "effeminate character" could serve as a source of temptation for the celibate monks.

Though the absence of carnal temptations is most likely the main motivator behind the peninsula's prohibition of women, most Athonite monks will claim otherwise. They are merely observers of an uncompromising rule laid down by the Blessed Mother herself. Dr. Graham Speake, author of *Mount Athos: Renewal in Paradis*, explained, "It's still called 'the garden of the mother of God,' dedicated to her glory, and she alone represents her sex on [the peninsula]." This rule was made even more cogent by the alleged succession of divine Marian apparitions that (conveniently) materialized before the Athonite monks in the years following the publication of the 1046 chrysobull. To this day, the only women allowed on the peninsula are the Virgin Mary and select female saints, captured in the frescoes of the Athonite monasteries.

Endless Battles

"The soul that has come to know God fully no longer desires anything else, nor does it attach itself to anything on this earth; and if you put before it a kingdom, it would not desire it, for the love of God gives such sweetness and joy to the soul that even the life of a king can no longer give it any sweetness." – Silouan the Athonite

The magnanimity the Byzantine rulers exhibited towards the Athonite monks has since been attributed to a number of political motivations. An unspoken rapport was forged between the royals and the monks, with the latter beholden to the emperors on account of their generous donations. The emperors further enhanced the relationship between them by gifting Athonite authorities sweeping territories in the Halkidiki outside of Athos, as well as in Thessaloniki, which became dependencies of the Athonite establishments.

Profits and goods produced by the monks' multiple dependencies ensured that their basic needs were fulfilled. For example, Athonites from the 12th century were reportedly so invested in the thriving wine trade in the Halkidiki, which was eventually woven into the peninsula's culture, that it incited great outcry from hordes of monks. Among the most vocal detractors of the monasteries' wine obsession was Efstathios, who served as the Archbishop of Thessaloniki between 1180 and 1195. He lamented, "[The Athonite monks] deliberate more on the vine than on theology."

Following the sack of Constantinople in 1204 during the Fourth Crusade in 1204, Mount Athos fell into the hands of the short-lived Frankish Kingdom of Thessaloniki ("Thessalonica"). This abrupt transition resulted in the loss of several Athonite properties outside of the peninsula, and though the kingdom was dissolved just 20 years later, they would not regain ownership of the properties in question until 1261, when the power of Constantinople was restored.

Once Mount Athos was again subjugated to the Byzantine Empire, local monks implored for peace, but regrettably, their prayers went unanswered. The obstinate Emperor Michael VIII Palaiologos was disliked by the Athonites from the very beginning, but it was his orchestration of the 1274 Union of Lyons, otherwise known as the "Second Council of Lyons," that most provoked the indignant wrath of the Athonite monks. His open persecution of the Athonite monks who objected to the council's verdict – which called for the end of the Great Schism that separated the Eastern Orthodox Church from the Roman Catholic Church – only aggravated the aggrieved monks.

Tensions between Emperor Michael VIII Palaiologos and the Athonites continued to decay, reaching a crescendo four years later when the emperor promulgated a decree that called for the marriage of these Churches at Constantinople, regardless of the permission of both parties. The reputation of John XI Bekkos, then the Ecumenical Patriarch of Constantinople, was no better; the holy man was branded a traitor by the Athonites when he voiced his support for the union.

A 14th century depiction of Emperor Michael VIII Palaiologos

After wrapping up their campaigns in the Holy Land, the Crusaders returned to Byzantine lands and pledged their services to Emperor Michael VIII Palaiologos. Turkish and Tartar soldiers-for-hire were also prepared to enforce Michael's proclamation, should the situation call for it.

The Athonites, as one might expect, were outraged by the authoritarian proclamation, and duly expressed their discontent in a withering letter. They wrote, "We clearly see that you [Emperor Michael] are becoming a heretic, but we implore you to forsake all this and abide in the teachings that were handed down to you...Reject the unholy and novel teachings of a false knowledge [in reference to the Latin Church], speculations, and additions to the Faith." They vehemently made clear their perpetual opposition against numerous doctrines upheld by the Catholic Church, such as the supremacy of and devotion displayed towards the pope, their distortion of the Holy Creed, and their utilization of "unleavened bread" as the Body of Christ, amongst other offenses.

The emperor bared his teeth, but the resolve of the Athonite monks did not waver, which only seemed to further incense the emperor. Indisposed to antagonizing his new Greek subjects, the prejudiced emperor – as portrayed by Orthodox sources – relieved his frustrations by tormenting the Bulgarian monks in the Zograf Monastery on the southwestern part of Mount Athos. In the autumn of 1284, a vicious contingent of armed Crusaders stormed into Zograf, presenting them with a chilling ultimatum: accept the Union of Lyons, or face the fatal consequences.

The Zograf Monastery

The spirits of the Zograf monks remained unbroken, but the better part of the brotherhood eventually filed out of the complex to avoid further hostilities. 26 held out in the monastery's tallest tower, and when the Catholic soldiers ordered them to vacate the premises once again, they refused to budge, seemingly resigned to their inevitable fates. On the 10th of October, the soldiers set the tower ablaze, and all 26 – including Friars Igumen Thomas, Cyril, Barsanuphius, Sava, Martinian, Cyprian, Parthenius, Joasaph, along with four other unnamed laymen – perished in the flames, giving their lives for the Orthodox cause.

The tempestuous relationship between the Catholics and Greek Orthodox remained as such until the latter part of the 14th century. Much of the relief is attributed to the Kydones brothers – elder brother, Demetrios, a wildly popular statesman who served three terms as *Mesazon* (Imperial Premier) for the Byzantine Empire, and younger brother, Prochoros, an Athonite monk and theologian. Together, the talented linguists converted a series of religious Latin texts into Greek, such as the *Mesazon*'s translation of Saint Thomas's *Summa contra Gentiles*. This passage from the *Dialogos Institute* illustrates what ensued: "[Demetrios] helped to bring about the reconciliation of...Emperor John V Palaiologos with the Holy See. In 1369, the Emperor and *Mesazon* traveled to Rome in person and professed the common faith of [the] east and west in Saint Peter's Basilica. Prochoros, a monk of Mount Athos, would later suffer persecution for his witness to the simplicity of the Godhead..."

The disagreements that developed within the monastic community on Mount Athos included the issue of being consecrated to a scholarly life on the peninsula. Initially, the majority of Athonite monks during this period found the growing treasury of texts impractical and pointless, if only because they were chiefly illiterate and educated only in the arts of austerity and spirituality gained through stringent self-discipline. It was only around the mid-14th century that this consensus faded. Athonite monks, encouraged by the influx of new, well-read monks, lowered their guards and began to dust off the precious literature in their monasteries. Not only did they begin to procure even more sacred manuscripts, a few monasteries – such as the Hilander and the Iveron – established *scriptoria* of their own and churned out their own texts. Soon, a cross-cultural network of intellectuals and creative spirits was developed within the peninsula, one colored by theologians, musical composers, hagiographers (biographers of saints), and ecclesiastical chroniclers. In addition to the Iveron and the Hilandar, the Panteleemon and Zograf Monasteries became vibrant academic hubs that functioned as distribution centers of religious texts to Bulgaria, Serbia, Georgia, and Russia.

The Iveron Monastery

It was during this time that the future Saint Gregory of Sinai, a displaced monk who made his home in Athos in 1310, divulged to the Athonites the mystical "Jesus prayer," a short incantation he learned from a Friar Arsenios in Crete: "Lord Jesus Christ, have mercy on me, a sinner." The charismatic Gregory managed to reel in a small, but ultimately high-yielding quantity of monks with the unconventional ideas of mysticism he peppered into his daily devotions, and he is therefore credited with introducing Hesychasm to the peninsula. Archbishop of Thessaloniki, esteemed theologian, and former Athonite monk Gregory Palamas heartily backed the esoteric teachings of Gregory of Sinai, and the trend of Hesychasm quickly gained traction, so much so that it was formally incorporated into the Orthodox doctrine in 1351.

Unfortunately, the blossoming prosperity of Mount Athos was bittersweet, because once their collections of literary gems and sacred relics continued to swell, unwanted attention from gluttonous outlanders increased accordingly. Callous convoys of marauding pirates from Asia Minor were among the first to descend upon Mount Athos between the late 12th century and early 13th century. The savage, sword-wielding pirates were so relentless that large bodies of Athonite monks began to teem out of the peninsula, seeking solace and refuge in the nearby cities of Meteora and Paroria instead. Moreover, the Byzantine Civil War, which dragged on between 1341 and 1347, saw the destruction of Thrace and Macedonia, along with the heinous slaughter of hundreds or perhaps even thousands of residents. Numerous Athonite monasteries suffered another spell of pillaging during this turbulent time.

In 1345, in the midst of the civil war, Serbian king Stefan Dušan captured the Macedonian city of Sérres and declared himself Emperor of the Serbs and Greeks. Stefan Uroš V, the heir to the imperial crown, went on to claim ownership of the peninsula, allotting different portions of the land to various divisions within the Serbian Empire. The crippled Byzantine authorities were disconcerted, to say the least, by the bold changes being made by the Serbians, but despite their best efforts, they were unable to reverse these actions. As such, the Serbian Empire continued to reign over Mount Athos until 1371.

To the disappointment of the Byzantine imperials, their control over Eastern Macedonia would soon collapse. Emperor John and his retinue scrambled to plug the holes rapidly sprouting along the sides of the sinking ship, which included an attempt to marshal an army with relics seized from the Athonite monasteries, but they failed to fend off the new, more menacing opponent on the horizon. In 1383, Ottoman Turkish forces conquered Sérres and seized Mount Athos soon thereafter.

As steadfastly faithful as the Athonites were to their principles, they knew it was time to recalibrate their defensive strategies. Fearing the loss of their monastic society altogether, the insightful monks went into survival mode. They had no delusions about their lackluster security – a sobering reality crystallized by their lack of defenses against the pirate attacks – and understood that their survival hinged on the protection and patronage of whoever bore the imperial crown. As narrated by a 16th century historian named "Muned/d/imbas/zi," a band of Orthodox representatives from the Pridromos Monastery near Sérres was assembled and sent to appeal to Sultan Orkhan (or Orhan) for an "*affirman*," or a guarantee of protection. The Athonite monks followed in their Macedonian brothers' footsteps years later, acquiring the guardianship and other privileges from Orkhan's successor, Sultan Murad I. Philotheos Kokkinos, who served as Ecumenical Patriarch of Constantinople for nearly three consecutive terms in the mid-14th century, confirmed the Ottomans' "support...and admiration," as well as the charity they exhibited towards the Athonite monks in his 1360 homily. This fruitful tactic, which entailed remaining in the good graces of those who posed the greatest threat, would not be lost on the future generations of Athonites.

Even with the Ottomans in their corner, Athonite monasteries saw a rather drastic decline in their population in the years leading up to the 1400s. This decline, many believe, led to the monasteries' gradual retirement of the cenobitic lifestyle. Instead, many Athonite institutions began to embrace the so-called "idiorrhythmic," or "self-regulating" system. Plainly put, while Athonite monks continued to belong to brotherhoods, they no longer lived collectively, but in privately-owned, often remotely situated cells. In addition to their new ability to obtain and maintain personal assets, a nostalgic sense of independence and true solitude was reinstated. Athonites who adhered to the idiorrhythmic system were expected to rear their own crops, secure their own supplies, repair their own clothes and furniture, and so forth. They spent the bulk of their days confined to their cells, only breaking away from their lodgings to attend services at a nearby *katholikon*. While the new monastic arrangement alienated many of the peninsula's residents, it also lured in a considerable number of aspiring monks from aristocratic backgrounds who were previously repelled by the rigidity of cenobitic monasticism.

By 1430, it was clear that the Ottomans were not going away anytime soon. In a surprising turn of events, however, the *Agion Oros* – which was, up to this point, seemingly under the permanent jurisdiction of the Turkish Sultan – was granted autonomy. In return, Athonite authorities agreed to surrender their territories in Macedonia and Thrace, as well as a few other privileges, and cough up a yearly tax for the continued protection of the Ottomans.

In the wake of the Ottomans' conquest of Constantinople and the dissolution of the Byzantine Empire, the Athonites continued to prosper under Turkish rule. Ottoman sultans and other affluent members of Turkish society began to entrust their valuables – mostly artwork, but some say, a few chests bursting with gold, silver, and jewels – to the Athonite monks, who carefully stowed them away in their monasteries for safekeeping. Apart from the compensation they received for the storage of said valuables, the most distinguished monasteries continued to be presented with regular donations. Monasteries dipped into their funds, further strengthening their fortifications.

The new commercial twists applied to Athonite customs solidified the new idiorrhythmic character that had developed within this small, free-form strip of land. Not only were monasteries accepting gratuities in exchange for prayers, blessings, and art-storage – even from those who had no intentions of visiting the monastery – Athonite institutions revived the viticultural trade and dabbled in other enterprises. For a parcel of land or a sum of 100 gold pieces, for instance, the monks pledged to provide their benefactors with predetermined quantities of wine, oil, cheese, legumes, wheat, tomatoes, peppers, and a host of other herbs and produce until the donor's death, delivered periodically and in batches. Though some complained about the impiety of making a profit, most made their peace with the practice, for they were, in their eyes, simply maximizing on surplus crops that would have otherwise gone to waste.

Furthermore, the increase in territorial and monetary donations resulted in the construction, as well as the structural and cosmetic rehabilitation of more monasteries on the peninsula. Among the reconditioned monasteries was Konstamonitou, a small, 10th-century compound funded in part by both Byzantine emperors and Serbian princes. The Konstamonitou was famous for its brick-red roof, its library of 100 rare codices, and for providing shelter to the icons of Saint Stephen and the *Panagia Hodgetria Antiphonetria.* Another was the Koutloumousiou. Originally founded in 1169, the square complex was renovated in the time of Abbot Chariton of Imbros, financed by a pair of Wallachian princes and other nobles along the Danube River. The *katholikon* of Koutloumousiou, dedicated to the Transfiguration of Christ, was constructed during the makeover, but was only embellished with frescoes in 1744. Today, the Koutloumousiou places sixth in the pyramid of Athonite monasteries.

The Konstamonitou

There were also some new monasteries raised, including the Monastery of Gregoriou, also known as the "Osiou Grigoriou Monastery." This triple-tiered, stern-looking stone structure was built upon a rocky protrusion right by the edge of the southwestern coast. It was designed in 1310 by Gregory the Young, the hesychast disciple of Saint Gregory of Sinai, and dedicated to Nicholas of Myra, the patron saint of sailors and merchants.

Rudolf Bauer's picture of the Osiou Grigoriou Monastery

The Monastery of Pantokratoros, between the Monasteries of Vatopedi and Iveron, was erected on the fringe of the peninsula's eastern coast in 1357. The complex, shaped like a slightly skewed trapezoid, was founded by two brothers known only as Alexios, *Megas Stratopedarches* (Grand Master of the Camp) for the Byzantine military, and John, the *Megas Primikerios* (Chief Lector of a Monastery). The Pantokrator, which originally harbored the Christ icon now displayed in St. Petersburg, boasted a handsome *katholikon* and 15 chapels. It quickly rose to prominence within the Athonite hierarchy, placing 15th by 1394.

The Pantokratoros

By the end of the 14th century, every monastery on the peninsula was sponsored by at least one wealthy noble. It became a tacit, but common practice for imperial and federal leaders to financially buttress one Athonite monastery apiece. These patrons saw it as a personal call of duty of sorts, for only then, they believed, could they ensure that their souls, along with those of their subjects, would be saved.

In 1424, the Athonites relied again on their diplomatic skills to shield themselves from the usual hassles and potential complications that typically came with a change in regime. That spring, a company of Athonite monks traveled to Adrianopolis ("Edirne") in East Thrace and successfully brokered another arrangement of patronage with Sultan Murad II. Ironically, the Athonites had sought the assent of Byzantine Emperor Manuel II Palaiologos prior to scheduling the meeting, but while the Athonites are most renowned for their homely, rustic lives, they were keenly aware of the stormy political climate and understood that they could not afford to lose any of their patrons, whether the patrons were Byzantine emperors, Ottoman nobles, or Danubian princes. Put simply, they strove to pave new paths, but they also made sure not to burn existing bridges.

There is plenty of evidence that showcases the continued camaraderie between the Athonites and Constantinople, even under Turkish rule. The Synod of Florence, otherwise known as the "Council of Florence," convened in that Italian city in between 1438 and 1439. A few weeks before the ecumenical conference, which was the Catholic Church's second attempt to merge with the Greek Orthodox, Emperor John VIII Palaiologos sent a team of delegates to Mount Athos for duplicates of reference codices and religious law books no longer available in Constantinople. The emperor also consulted with Athonite elders, and he was so dependent on their wisdom that he invited an assemblage of monks to the council to represent the Byzantine side.

The growing popularity of Hesychasm on Mount Athos, however, split the Orthodox Christians of 14th century Byzantine society. One camp praised the mystic system, and the other stigmatized the practice as bizarre and sinfully occult. The fundamentals of this system are briefly described in the following passage from Mitchell B. Liester's *Hesychasm: A Christian Path of Transcendence*: "[Hesychasts (practitioners of Hescyhasm)] encouraged individual experiences of the divine...[Hesychasts] describe two types of consciousness: ego-centered and ego-transcendent. The former is a state dominated by attachments to the senses, emotions, intellect, and imagination. The latter involves detachment from those faculties...The ultimate goal for Hesychasts is union with God."

Liester expands on the three steps required to reach this goal: "The first is dispassion (*apatheia*), which involves detachment from the senses and the emotions. The second is stillness (*hesychia*), which requires detachment from the discursive intellect and the imagination. The final step is an abiding state of illumination called 'deification' or 'perfect union with God' (*theosis*)."

Advocates, mainly from the Greek portion of the Eastern Church, defended the system, citing its alignment with the gospel revealed by the "apparitions of divine light" during the Transfiguration on Mount Tambor. Dialogue surrounding the delicate subject was conducted on three separate Synods – the Councils of 1341, 1347, and 1351 - but since the system had the backing of the Byzantine emperors themselves, Hesychasm triumphed on all three occasions. In the years that followed, a wave of Hesychast practitioners, including Gregory Palamas, Makarios Makris, Germanos the Athonite, among others, were proclaimed saints by the Orthodox Church.

The Floating Monasteries of Meteora

"Pull all by yourself and as hard as you can the rope which lifts your little basket up to your most intimate Meteora." – Odysseas Elytis, 20th century writer

In 1336, Byzantine Emperor Andronikos III Palaiologos published a *chrysobullos logos*, or chrysobull. The prized parchment, which boasted a golden seal and royal-purple tassels, not only reiterated all the monastic privileges and guarantees of protection granted to the Hilander Monastery on Mount Athos a few years earlier, but confirmed the donation of the St. George Monastery in Thessaly to a hieromonk (a monk ordained into the priesthood) named Kallinikos. Moreover, the boundaries of the Bishopric of Stagoi were described and validated, and the monasteries within the district placed under the imperial wing.

A contemporary portrait of Emperor Andronikos III Palaiologos

This chrysobull, another pivotal milestone that propelled Meteora's reputation as sacred ground to even greater heights, has since been immortalized in the form of a verbatim inscription etched unto the northern walls of the inner antechamber within the Chapel of Dormition of Theotokos. Visitors will also find the words of the *sigilio* (an official edict issued by the Orthodox Patriarch) proclaimed by Patriarch Antonios IV in 1393 carved onto the walls. The document emphasized the Byzantine emperors' universal sovereignty over all "lesser kings and princes," and it itemized the liberties and entitlements granted to the monasteries and churches within the Bishopric of Stagoi.

Not long before the unveiling of the 1336 chrysobull, Emperor Andronikos III Palaiologos raised a small town he named "Kouveltsi" on the fertile banks of the River Lithaiou, just a little over 3 miles away from Stagoi. Kouveltsi, referenced in the chrysobull, was renamed "Theopetra Kalambakas" as an homage to the Theopatra Cave ("The Stone That Touched God"), which hovered over the town on the northeastern part of a 591-ft-tall limestone rock formation called the "Muti."

The town's population blossomed in the centuries that followed, luring pious people who did not necessarily wish to immerse themselves in monasticism, but who wanted to experience a taste of the renowned tranquility. The allure of urban life eventually reclaimed many of its residents, as only 600 remain in Theopetra Kalambakas today, where their trade is chiefly centered on agriculture and animal breeding. That being said, residents continue to uphold the religious traditions passed down to them by their ancestors. During Holy Week, for instance, the town's young people take to the forest to collect timber, holly, and other kindling for a roaring bonfire on the pinnacle of the Theopetra Rock. The flames, otherwise known as the "Great Fire," pierce the dark of the night with a dancing, golden glow on the evening of the Resurrection. The following morning, the villagers gather in the town square, celebrating with joyous prayers and folk dances, clad in colorful traditional costumes.

The Theopetra Rock

As the the 14th century drew to a close, the fragile harmony in Greece was shattered by the conquest of almost all Byzantine strongholds by the Ottoman Turks. The Ottoman Empire, as noted by *Oxford Islamic Studies,* posed "a major threat to the hegemony of Christian Europe from the 14th to the 17th centuries." The Ottomans were, more precisely, Seljuk Turks who are believed to have first appeared in the northwestern neck of Anatolia. Owing to the proximity of the nascent, but wildly promising Ottoman Empire to the inadequately guarded territories of the Byzantine Empire, the dauntless Turks infiltrated and ultimately seized Byzantine lands with considerable ease. In addition to the strategic placement of Ottoman strongholds, the Turks were skilled in combat, and evidently they proved adept at the art of negotiation, recruiting both oppressed Muslims who resented the Byzantine Christian authorities and converts.

It was in 1338 that the Turks first ousted the Byzantines from Anatolia, and just 16 years later, the Turks conquered Gallipoli, the southern part of East Thrace, securing their first stronghold in Eastern Europe. With every victory, their confidence and ambitions grew, and the Turks subsequently unleashed a spate of military campaigns and raids upon various cities in southern Europe.

Much to the disappointment of the Turks, the castles and fortresses under the umbrella of the Byzantine Empire were hastily informed about the incoming invasions and given the order to strengthen their fortifications at once. Affluent Greek cities, which were (correctly) rumored to be bursting with treasure, soon found themselves in the crosshairs of the Ottoman forces. Like the other Byzantine domains, local authorities buttressed their bulwarks, marshaled more soldiers, and doubled the stock of their granaries and armories. Failing to acquire much steam against the Greek castles, the Turks eventually decided to redirect their endeavors to the land's monasteries instead. The Greek monasteries were sheltered by the imperial shield, but with the remoteness of the monasteries' location, particularly that of Mount Athos (the largest monastic community in Greece), it was to a far lesser extent. The strictly non-violent nature of the monks only enhanced the Turks' attraction towards the monasteries, which, at this time, began to double as storage rooms for the valuables of multiple emperors, princes, and aristocrats.

By this time, the Athonite monasteries, along with the residences along the coasts of the Chalkidike region, were no strangers to attacks, especially those carried out by pirates and the mercenaries of the Catalan Grand Company. However, it was becoming increasingly difficult to stave off the multiplying Turkish intrusions in the mid-14th century, and their outdated defenses were no match for the growingly sophisticated, organized, and continuously expanding Turkish navy. The trespassers stayed put until the monks caved in, and usually they only left once they had a signed document outlining a tribute agreement. These agreements typically mandated that the monasteries pay the Turks every year.

An account from an Athonite monk named Païsios documents the pressure that the peninsula's monks were burdened with as a result of these annual tributes. To begin with, the Athonite abbots chose to keep mum about the real number of monks there, so as to lessen the taxes they were expected to pay each year. At one point, there were over 6,000 monks on the sacred peninsula, but only 4,000 were listed in the papers submitted to the Turks. The following excerpt, from A. Vacalopoulos' "History of Macedonia 1354-1833," explains the effects of these debilitating tributes: "[The Athonite monks] were also obliged to pay in cash 1/7th of the value of their yield in wheat, barley, oats, peas, green-vegetables, and grapes, but this at twice the reigning market-prices. All products derived from fishing were subject to the same tax. For the larger animals that they pastured on the various summer and winter pasturages [sic], they were obliged to pay five Turkish coins...per head; while for the smaller animals, such as sheep and goats, and for every beehive, they paid three coins. But this was not the end of their tax burdens – they were subject to a variety of other minor taxes besides..."

Unfortunately, despite the Athonites' tactics and the abbots' best efforts, by the end of the 14th century, the 300 or so monasteries on Mount Athos had dwindled to a mere 35. The monks who decamped, for the most part, had had enough of the discomfort, vulnerability, and financial stresses brought about by the incessant raids and threats.

Throughout this time, monks who owned land faced the brunt of the perils, as their isolated properties were violated not only by pirates, but also by the *Sipahi,* the name given to Ottoman fief-holding cavalrymen. Others were turned off by the heightening hostilities displayed by the panicking and therefore short-tempered *protas* of the Athonite monasteries, as well as the worsening disputes regarding the borders of monastic estates. Many of those who elected to stay behind did their best to preserve the estates and worked doubly hard to produce the funds and yield the crops required for the taxes, but when the weight of their debts and responsibilities became too much bear, they, too, were forced to vacate.

In time, many of the former monks of Mount Athos either applied for lodgings at other Greek monasteries or gave up the practice altogether and sought refuge among the civilians of nearby villages and cities. However, a trinity of monks from the Athonite Monastery of Iviron – Moses, Gregory, and Athanasios Koinovitis (future Saint Athanasios the Meteorite) - forged ahead on an entirely different course. Following a particularly ferocious ambush on the Monastery of Iviron, the historic trio packed up their belongings in the autumn of 1340 and embarked on a quest to raise a monastery of their very own. Enticed by the stories of the spectacular miracles that allegedly transpired on the Thessalian plains, as well as the riveting tales of the unblemished cave-chapels and monastic communities around Meteora's rock pillars, the monks headed towards Stagoi. Only upon their arrival did it dawn on them that they had found an ideal location; the peaks of the rock columns may have been treacherous, but the monks were undeterred by the heights, which offered a perfect place that was secluded, peaceful, and inaccessible by unwelcome visitors and outsiders in general. Captained by Athanasios, the three monks clambered up to the flat crest of a medium-sized rock pillar called "Stylo ton Stagon," or "Stylos" for short. There, the monks erected small, single-room shacks for themselves, as well as a miniature Orthodox temple that they christened the "Church of the Panayia Meteoritissa Petra." These structures were, as declared by Athanasios on the day of the their consecration, "place[d] under the roof of the Blessed Virgin Mary...which is the [sole] purpose of this monastery." It was upon the Stylos peak that Athanasios organized the "systematic *koenovion,*" putting in place the monastic guidelines, beliefs, and missions of a new generation in Meteora.

About three or four years later, Athanasios rappelled down from the Stylos pinnacle, his eyes fixated upon the one that dwarfed the rest of the rock pillars: the Playts Lithos ("Broad Rock"). Here, he oversaw the construction of yet another monastic community – the Monastery of the Transfiguration – equipping the new complex with separate residential cells, as well as a chapel in a small cave on the cliff face.

Future generations were stumped by Athanasios' ability to scramble up the towering rock unassisted, and they were even more perplexed by how he managed to lug up the building materials required for the monastery, which stood at a height of over 2,000 feet above sea level. Thus, local legends claimed that he had tamed a tremendous heaven-sent eagle, which he then mounted and piloted towards the unreachable pinnacle. In reality, Athanasios, as maintained by historians, was accompanied by an assortment of 14 Athonite and local monks. They did not scurry up the pillar with supernatural help; instead, they punched holes into one side of the pillar's facade, fitted the man-made cavities with stacked beams, and used the scaffolding they had created to reach the peak.

Some say that the sensational panoramic view of the lofty pillars and rugged landscape, carpeted with ravishing forests, provided the inspiration for the name of the heavenly rock columns for the first time. Before this, the pillars and their monasteries apparently lacked a collective appellation, but now, Athanasios declared it was to be known as the "Megalo Meteoro," meaning the "Great Place Suspended/Floating in the Air." The name later evolved to "Meteoron," then to "Meteoros," and finally shortened to "Meteora." Athanasios is also said to have affectionately referred to the columns as the "City of Stone."

Possibly persuaded by his second wife, Maria Palaiologina (the daughter of Byzantine prince John Palaiologos), the Serbian Emperor of Thessaly, Symeon Uroš, presented Athanasios with the funds in 1356 to construct a *katholikon,* or central church, upon the Platys Lithos. This became the Church of the Transfiguration of Christ. The Monastery of the Transfiguration, also known as the "Great Meteoron," also benefited from the emperor's patronage, as part of the funds procured were set aside for renovations and expansions. The Great Meteoron, was at this stage, among, if not the most secure of all the monasteries in Greece. Not only could the monks retract their semi-collapsible ladders when danger was on the horizon, the monastic community was unaffected by the political insurgencies and other tribulations faced by the rest of society.

The Great Meteoron was aptly named, for it continues to reign as the largest, oldest, and most highly elevated of the surviving Meteoran monasteries. Prior to the construction of Meteoron's *katholikon,* the monks had to squeeze into the cramped cave-chapel to carry out their daily devotions. A small courtyard was also installed within the plain, original monastery, where exhausted monks could cool off under the shade of the fruit trees after their grueling ascents to the top. Following the modernization and expansion of the Great Meteoron, the compound had swelled to about 50 acres in size.

A modern picture of the Great Meteoron

The monasteries were initially only accessible by ladders measuring 40 feet long that the monks pulled out when needed, but around 1520, the loft of the so-called "Great Meteoron Tower" was fitted with a net "hitched over a hook," which was then lowered to the ground via a pulley system. Others used durable baskets to hoist themselves up and down the mighty pillar. It wasn't until 1923 that a stone staircase consisting of 146 steep steps was constructed to lead to the Great Meteoron's entrance. The net is still utilized by the aging monks as a manual dumbwaiter of sorts, transporting goods much too heavy for them to manually carry. Winding lengths of steel cables and cable cars were added later to make it easier for Meteoran priests and monks to access the other Meteoran monasteries.

In 1370, John Uros inherited the Thessalian throne from his father, Emperor Symeon, but after only three years, he voluntarily surrendered the imperial crown and scepter to his nobleman cousin, a Byzantine Greek native named Alexios Angelos Philanthropenos. A few years later, in the spring of 1373, the former emperor renounced the extravagant luxuries and seductive power that came with the imperial lifestyle and became a brother of the Great Meteoron Monastery, taking up the name "Ioasaph" (also spelled "Joasaph") at his induction.

When Athanasios the Meteorite passed on in 1383, the torch was passed on to none other than Brother Joasaph. Throughout the remaining 40 years of Joasaph's life at the Great Meteoron, he picked up from where his predecessor had left off, launching a new round of upgrades and expansions, including the addition of a new monastic building that housed more residential cells, as well as cistern and its own hospital. The *katholikon* was also refurbished under Joasaph's guidance. The final design of the Church of the Transfiguration is best encapsulated in this short passage from Christine Boutsia's article, "Great Meteoron Monastery: The Holy Monastery of the Great Meteoro." The article notes, "The *[katholikon]* has a Greek-cross-in-square floor plan, with a 12-sided central dome resting on a drum following the architectural Athonic type..." The *katholikon* underwent another round of cosmetic touch-ups and enlargements from late 1544 to early 1545 in an effort to repair the damages incurred from a terrible earthquake in the summer of 1544.

The *katholikon* of the Great Meteoron is arguably the most splendid basilica in all of Meteora. The interior of the structure, segregated into four sections – the exonarthex, narthex, sanctuary, and nave – bore a striking contrast to its unadorned, peach-roofed exterior. Its walls were used as canvases for brilliant fresco masterpieces painted in the classic 15th century Macedonian style, defined by vivid color palettes, the minimalistic, yet lifelike facial features of its human subjects, and the perfectly disc-shaped, gilded halos, bordered in white or black, painted around the heads of Christian saints and martyrs.

Christ Pantocrator (Christ the Almighty), a portrait of a bearded Jesus, is among the most notable subjects of the Meteoron frescoes. Naturally, symbolism lay behind every meticulously planned feature of Christ's countenance. His broad and curved forehead hinted at His wisdom, and his slender, slightly hooked nose was symbolic of His spiritual nobility. His wide, piercing eyes stared straight into the windows of one's soul, and His thin, pursed lips suggested the "silence of contemplation." In His left arm, He clutched a thick book bound in orange leather, the Book of the Gospels. His free hand is gently raised midway, with His pointer and middle finger extended, and the remaining pressed against His thumb, blessing anyone who paid tribute to the portrait. Other subjects include the *Virgin Enthroned* and the *Three Hierarchs,* as well as a selection of scenes from the life of Christ and the portraits of Athanasios, Joasaph, and numerous "military saints."

The frescoes that covered the walls of the *katholikon's* narthex were especially enthralling. The ghastly scenes of lynching, the roasting of human flesh, and other grisly tortures inflicted upon early Christian martyrs were as captivating as they were chilling. The barbaric punishments suffered by the damned souls in the *Last Judgment* section added to the morbid theatricality of the place.

The walls opposite these frescoes featured full-length depictions of the founders, as well as paintings of John the Baptist and famous Meteoran saints. They were juxtaposed with more amicable imagery, such as the Baptism of the Christ, as well as the First and Seventh Ecumenical Councils. The refectory, or dining room, located on the northern part of the *katholikon*, was renovated in 1557. The vaulted roof, shored up by five pillars, was patched up, and the apse was brightened up with paintings of the archangels Gabriel and Michael, as well as the Blessed Virgin. Different crews were also dispatched to maintain and rehabilitate the Grand Meteoron's three chapels – the Chapel of St. Athanasios, the Chapel of St. John the Baptist, and the Chapel of Saints Constantine and Helena – when needed.

While the internal splendor of the Great Meteoron continued to burgeon, succored by the independence it was granted by the Patriarch of Constantinople in 1415, the humility of the monks who resided there did not waver. The prominence of the complex reached its crescendo in the 16th century, when its visitors grew exponentially and it was presented with donation after donation from emperors, princes, and wealthy peers seeking blessings from the monks. Thanks to these contributions, the monastic complex gained a new kitchen, an even larger refectory, a revamped defensive tower, a private hospice, and a home for the elderly.

Eventually, the close-knit community nurtured by the monks of the Great Meteoron rendered it among the first official cenobitic monasteries of Meteora. Meteoron monks did not sleep in closely spaced, individual huts, but rather, in separate rooms under one roof. The monks were expected to abide by a set schedule, and to execute chores and other duties shared amongst themselves. For example, the monks required to appear at church no less than four times a day to complete Orthodox liturgical sessions that lasted roughly six hours in total. They also dined together, either twice or three times a day, at the refectory, solemnly consuming their identical meals at a lengthy wooden dining table that measured a whopping 100 feet across.

The library of the Great Meteoron was a trove of treasures of a different kind, and the following are only some of the literary jewels that were located there: "Manuscripts, Byzantine and post-Byzantine documents, books concerning the function of the monastery, patristic [sic] texts, hymnographical texts, rare incunabula of the 15th -19th centuries [totaling 450 volumes], a collection of music and legal manuscripts and ancient texts [penned by] Homer, Sophocles, Demosthenes, Hesiod, Aristotle, and other Alexandrian writers..." Between the 16th and 17th centuries, the library was partitioned to host a bibliographic workshop, and some monks worked as scribes, producing hagiographies and replicating ancient manuscripts. Another workshop in the monastery was devoted to weaving and embroidery. Nimble-fingered needle-workers spun cloths and lined their edges with gold thread. Embroidered epitaphs of deceased monks were also fabricated.

Many of the facilities utilized by the medieval monks are still in use to this day. The walls of the kitchen next to the refectory are still stained with smoke and ash. The old brick bread oven (where the monks boiled soup) and wine cellar, stocked with barrels of homemade wine, baskets of fresh crops, and agricultural equipment, also remain and have yet to be upgraded.

The ossuary, which many consider the most intriguing part of the complex, is yet another amenity still in operation today. This cave-like chamber, enclosed with coarse walls of stone and brick, was the final resting place for the monks who had passed on. In lieu of traditional caskets, the skulls and select bones of the "founding fathers" of Great Meteoron were enshrined in a door-less cabinet hewn out of timber. Each shelf was neatly lined with yellowed, centuries-old skulls, save for the bottom and topmost shelves. The skulls on the bottom shelf were nestled among piles of bones, whereas the top shelf was reserved for dusty portraits of the same founding fathers. A small candelabrum with half-used wicks, an ornate dangling candle holder rimmed by scarlet stained glass, and the small, crudely carved window provide this otherwise dark room with some illumination.

Interestingly, while the Great Meteoron is now considered the highest of all the Meteoran monasteries, this wasn't always the case. Visitors who head over to the windows on the southeastern wing of the monastery can get a view of the Ypselotera Pillar next door. The Ypselotera Peak, nicknamed the "Highest of the Heavens," dominates even the Platys Lithos, and was once home to the lesser-known Ypselotera Monastery. Not much is known about this peak-perching compound apart from the fact that it was founded in 1390. Ultimately, the dubious living conditions and the miserably difficult climb up to Ypselotera resulted in its abandonment sometime in the mid-1600s. Today, there are still ruins, along with the broken, rotting ladder that once led to this long-defunct monastery.

The second largest monastery after the Great Meteoron is one that calls itself the "Holy Monastery of Varlaam" (also spelled "Barlaam"). The monastery was named after the founder of the original complex, an ascetic monk and contemporary of Athanasios named Varlaam, who scaled the pillar in 1350. On this spot, he established three churches, a water tank, and a small shack for himself.

The Holy Monastery of Varlaam

The location was packed with potential, but few others at the time seemed to recognize it. Following the death of Varlaam in the early 15th century, the empty monastery fell into disuse, occupied only by cobwebs, but in 1517, two brother monks, Theophanes and Nektarios Asparades of Yiannena, took it upon themselves to rehabilitate the abandoned compound. The Asparades brothers were deeply devout nobles who chose to immerse themselves in monasticism from an early age, receiving much of their education at the Monastery of Philanthropinon in the Greek city of Ioannina. They later found a mentor in Savvas, an elder who belonged to the Hermitage of the Honorable Forerunner. Savvas appointed them "schemamonks" in 1495, a title defined by *Orthodox Wiki*: "The *schema* goes beyond carrying the Cross of Christ...he must be willing to surrender his life to totally save people's souls." Not long after the death of their mentor in 1505, the brothers moved to Mount Athos, and they remained in the Dionysiou Monastery for some time before returning to Ioannina.

The Monastery of Varlaam was not their first renovation project. In 1507, they completed an overhaul of a deserted cave dwelling in Ioannina that was once inhabited by an ascetic hermit for 18 years. Evidently, the brothers were also well-versed in diplomacy, for they managed to secure the enthusiastic support of Patriarch Pachomios I. By the end of their endeavors, they had raised the fully-furnished Church of the Honorable Forerunner, as well as a number of cells and other necessary facilities. The brothers went on to construct the Hermitage of St. Nicholas in Lepenos, which was occupied by their equally pious parents and sisters, and this complex would later become a dependency of the Monastery of Varlaam.

Like Athanasios and the founders of the other Meteoran monasteries, Theophanes and Nektarios were eventually displaced by external forces, but instead of being harassed by pirates and the Turkish *sipahi*, the Asparades brothers were singled out and endlessly badgered by religious and secular authorities. The nature of their conflicts is unknown, for the brothers neglected to disclose the real reasons behind the disagreements in their joint autobiography, but whatever the case, the suffering brothers sought out Patriarch Nephon for advice. Patriarch Nephon told them, "When temptations overwhelm us, do not withstand it, but withdraw from the monastery and gain peace." Taking his advice to heart, the brothers left their home of four years and traveled to Meteora in search of a new home. There, they courteously requested the permission from the *protas* of the Great Meteoron, as well as the Metropolitan Bessarion of Larissa, to reside in the unoccupied Monastery of Varlaam on a stone column now known as the "Pillar of the Honorable Father."

Once they determined that the decayed buildings of the derelict Monastery of Varlaam could no longer be salvaged, the brothers tore down the crumbling buildings and were essentially forced to start from scratch. Following the erection of their living quarters – two restored cells – they went to work on the rebuilding of Varlaam's Church of the Three Hierarchies. The Holy Altar, the only partial survivor of the original structure, was refinished. The finger of Saint John the Baptist, as well as the bone taken from the shoulder blade of Saint Andrew – the relics used in the original consecration of the *katholikon* – were also returned to its rightful place. Like the founding fathers of the Great Meteoron, the Asparades brothers and the rest of the builders employed scaffolding, as well as pulley and net systems to haul up building materials from the ground. The monks of the Monastery of Varlaam relied on strong ladders, baskets, and nets to transport themselves up and down the pillar.

The unique frescoes inside the *katholikon* of Varlaam were the original works of a Theban artist named Franco Catelano, who painted these pieces in early 1548. Catelano's remarkable and inimitable style and technique are brilliantly embodied in the frescoes coating the walls and portals, brought to life with rich, warm hues, fantastical creatures, and the emotive expressions of the human subjects. Other priceless treasures in this monastery are hoarded in the sacristy, which contains a coveted collection of "relics, manuscripts, portable icons, items in silver and other metals, gold-embroidered vestments," and more.

The first round of renovations was completed in the early autumn of 1517 or 1518, and the Asparades brothers moved in permanently that October. For the next seven years, the brothers remained on this cliff, but they had to evacuate for increasingly longer periods at a time due to the dreadful weather. The brothers continued to reside in the Monastery of Varlaam sporadically until after the completion of the *katholikon* in 1542, but ultimately they took the blustery winds and torrential downpours as omens indicating that they had worn out their welcome, so they duly left the pillar for good. The Monastery of Varlaam, it seems, was a true test of one's resilience; today, no more than seven monks are left in the monastery.

Another noteworthy Meteoran monastery is the Holy Monastery of Aghia Triada, also known as the "Monastery of the Holy Trinity." Situated on a lonesome pillar wedged between a pair of ravines, the cluster of partially wooden buildings, tiled with blood-orange roofs and fenced in by cyprus trees, is now accessible by 130 stone steps, a section of which passes through a tunnel bored into the rock. Though the monastery was referencedas early as 1362 in a proclamation issued by Greek-Serbian Emperor Symeon Oursesis Palaiologos, the construction of the *katholikon* only began in 1476.

Napoleon Vier's picture of the Monastery of the Holy Trinity

The circular, "rock-hewn" Chapel of Timios Prodromos (St. John the Forerunner), which connected to the passage leading to the courtyard, was consecrated to St. John the Baptist in 1682. The frescoes that covered every inch of the chapel's rocky walls, from top to bottom, as well as those that graced every face and corner of the arches, walls, ceilings, and pillars within the *katholikon*, are the work of two 18th century brothers, Friars Antonios and Nicolaos. They have aged over the centuries, but the timeless beauty of the art remains immaculate.

Given its hazardous position on the imposing clifftop, the Monastery of Aghia Triada is believed to be the least visited of all the monastic complexes, but fans of action classics might have spotted this glorious monastery during the climactic closing scenes of the 1981 James Bond film, *For Your Eyes Only*. Today, the Monastery of the Holy Trinity is host to two dependencies, the Holy Monastery of Aghios Nikolaos Bandovas and the Holy Monastery of Aghios Antonios. Maintenance and refurbishments of these complexes are arranged by the parent monastery.

By the 15th century, a complicated variety of factors, mainly the injustices suffered by the Christian public at the hands of the Ottoman rulers, led to a substantial upswing in the population of Meteora. Following the Islamic conquest of Greece in the mid-15th century, Christians and Jews alike were singled out and diminished to subordinate, second-class citizens, otherwise known as *"dhimmi* status." Being painted with such a mark meant that one was forbidden from spreading the religion on any Islamic terrain, and those who defied this crucial law were immediately put to their deaths.

It was no secret that the remodeled system was designed against the Christians. They were prohibited from applying for "mid-tier" professions and toting weapons, so as to keep them virtually penniless, and then made to shell out taxes that outweighed those paid by their Muslim counterparts. Many of those unable to foot the bills resorted to selling off their children as slaves. Tensions amongst the Christians themselves were also on the climb, with the more religious vilifying their Christian brothers and sisters who decided to abandon the faith.

It was not merely their rights that were trampled upon, as non-Muslim voices were muted, too. Not only were all testimonies of Christians against Muslims instantly tossed out of the courtroom, crimes and injustices suffered by Christians fell on the deaf ears of Muslim authorities.

By the end of the 16th century, a total of 24 monasteries, each of which consisted of at least one *katholikon*, a number of residential cells, and a refectory, had been erected in the magnificent stone forest of Meteora, making it the second largest monastic community in all of Greece after the blessed Mount Athos. Needless to say, as the site grew, the customs that bound together the Meteoran monks continued to evolve, and one of the most fascinating aspects of the rapidly developing culture was the unique penalty system developed by these resourceful monks. Meteoran monks found guilty of misconduct were banished to the caves of the "prison pillars," where they spent years repenting and atoning for their sins. The *Fylakes Kalogeron*, or "Monks' Jail," was one such place of confinement, where monks served their time in a spacious, but dreary cave nearly 200 feet above ground level. Others were put in a cave within the Rock of the Holy Spirit, a cragged, solitary formation reminiscent of a fat shark tooth. The prison cave was cited in *The Ladder of Divine Ascent*, authored by Saint John Climacus of Sinai, where he was sentenced for a period of one month. John, like the rest of the "convicts," was shackled and escorted to the cave via scaffolding, after which the scaffolding was then disassembled, leaving the imprisoned monks stranded.

Contrary to what one might imagine, despite the alienation from the rest of society (which ascetic monks had grown accustomed to anyways) and the negative connotations attached to these "prison caves," the experience wasn't all that bad. The following passage, written by John, almost likens the experience to an extended peaceful retreat: "A soul that has lost its one-time confidence and abandoned its hope of dispassion, that has broken the seal of chastity, that has squandered the treasury of divine graces, that has become a stranger to divine consolation, that has rejected the Lord's command...and that is wounded and pierced by sorrow as it remembers all this, will not only take on the labors mentioned above with all eagerness, but will even decide devoutly to kill itself with penitential works. It will also do so if there is in it only the tiniest spark of love or fear of the Lord..."

The usage of these prison pillars may have also been revived by the Turkish-Albanian invaders who entered the area in the latter half of the 1700s.

Fascinating Friars

"When there is a respect for small things, there will be an even greater respect towards the bigger things." – attributed to Saint Paisios of Athos

To the monks on Mount Athos, prayer is life. Prayers and incantations were quite literally injected into every waking minute of their day. For starters, Athonite monks attended tediously rambling services that lasted anywhere between 5-8 hours a day, all 365 days of the year. Services were customarily prolonged on special feast days and religious celebrations; on Christmas, for example, the Athonite monks cooped themselves up in their churches for at least 15 consecutive hours.

The interior of the Athonite *katholikon*, the heart and soul of these monasteries, is breathless, consisting of ornate, gilded candelabras, majestic frescoes, priceless portraits, and intricate gold-leaf embellishments. The aromatic fragrance of frankincense and a medley of other nuances, emanating from the *livani* (Orthodox incense sticks) only elevates the sense of serenity. It was inside of these striking churches that the Athonite monks spent the better part of their days.

Most of the Athonite monasteries scheduled their services in the evening, sometimes as late as 2:00 a.m., because the more deafening the silence, the more effective their prayer. Towards the end of service, it was tradition for one of the higher-ranking monks to present to the congregation a number of the monastery's most prized relics, encased in separate silver reliquaries. Members of the brotherhood, as well as present pilgrims, formed a queue, with each granted an opportunity to plant a kiss on these miracle-inducing relics.

To this day, no modern instruments or backing tracks are used in Athonite services. Not only do modern monks find the usage of such accompaniments distracting, they strive to parallel their lives with those of the saints and martyrs of past centuries. As a result, most Athonites use only their voices to create music, which have made them master harmonizers, and instruments from the Byzantine era are used periodically. Moreover, only hymns from centuries-old songbooks are chorused.

The unceasing praying also continues outside of their respective *katholikon*, as the lips of an Athonite are perpetually dancing with monotonous, under-the-breath chants. Most recite either the "Jesus Prayer" or "*Kyrie eleison*" ("Lord, have mercy"). The habit is so deeply embedded among even the modern Athonite monks that they are able to wordlessly mouth these chants as they perform their daily duties.

Incessant praying aside, Athonite monks throughout history kept themselves preoccupied with the daily tasks and roles assigned to them, usually by the abbots. Cenobitic and idiorrhythmic monks alike were typically given positions that corresponded with their fortes, as well as a series of jobs, known collectively as *diakonimata* (obedience/offerings), that they were expected to complete weekly. Those with a knack for the culinary arts were appointed cooks, while wordsmiths were appointed scribes, hagiographers, and historical chroniclers. Those gifted with green thumbs were made managers of gardens and vineyards. The medically trained became doctors and worked out of small clinics in the monasteries. Daily tasks included beekeeping, fishing, and carpentry, as well as cleaning and maintenance work. They were, in sum, self-sufficient.

A separate department was created for the preservation and cataloging of the artwork and relics the monasteries had amassed. All in all, the Athonite monasteries are estimated to have procured a staggering 20,000 icons and 15,000 manuscripts, as well as dozens upon dozens of cabinets overflowing with costly crucifixes, bejeweled chalices, exquisite embroidery, and other irreplaceable fortunes.

The monks' distinctive dietary habits also separated the Athonites from the rest of the Greek Orthodox monks. To begin with, the Athonite brothers of the Byzantine Era were among the first to practice what can partially be described as "intermittent fasting," about 200 days each year. On Tuesdays, Thursdays, Saturdays, and Sundays, classified as "non-fasting days," the monks ate twice a day (once at about 11:00 a.m., and again at around 7:00 p.m.). On "abstention," or "fasting days," they ate only once, usually at dusk. On these days, their simple meals were restricted to plates of vegetables, fruit, lentils, or plain bread, and wine, milk, cheese, and the use of olive oil were to be avoided. All Athonite monks were either strict vegetarians or pescatarians.

Three "knocks" on the *semantron* – usually an unadorned percussion instrument reminiscent of a paddle, found in the arcade – summoned the Athonite monks to the refectory. They ate for only 10 minutes at a time, wolfing down their meals and downing the wines in their goblets in complete silence. There was no chit-chat allowed, because they were instead supposed to listen intently to the prayers or hagiographies recited by an elder monk. Only on non-abstention days were the monks allowed fish fried in olive oil, complete with a side of vegetables consisting of garden-fresh herbs.

The season of Great Lent is regarded as the most significant fasting period in the Orthodox Church, and Angelos Rentoulas noted the importance of this season in his 2016 article, "Fasting and Feasting on Mount Athos." "This is a period of preparation for Christians, both spiritual and physical, an exercise in spiritual upliftment which helps purify them so they can celebrate the feast of the Resurrection." Athonite chefs made certain to tweak their cooking methods in accordance with the rules of Athonite abstention during these 40 days. For example, they replaced olive oil with *tahini* (sesame paste), and only certain shellfish and mollusks were consumed on Great Lent.

Perhaps unsurprisingly, more often than not, Athonite monks had extremely clean bills of health and frequently outlived the laymen in the mainland. Researchers who were intrigued by the monks' disciplined diets conducted a study on the physical conditions of the Athonite monks.

A total of 1,500 monks participated in the study between the years of 1994 and 2007. Of the 1,500 monks, not a single one tested positive for bowel or lung cancer, and only 11, representing 0.73% of the subjects, were diagnosed with prostate cancer. Haris Aidonopoulos, a urologist at the University of Thessaloniki, explained, "What seems to be the key is a diet that alternates between olive oil and non-olive oil days, and plenty of plant proteins. It's not only what we call the 'Mediterranean diet,' but also eating the old-fashioned way. Simple meals at regular intervals are very important."

The millennium-old diet is only one reason the Athonites live longer. After all, monks on the peninsula are afforded plenty of exercise thanks to the manual labor of harvesting ripe crops, kneading bread, transporting hefty building materials, and other daily tasks. Furthermore, the voluntary seclusion of the Athonite monks has shielded them from the stress that came with the ills of the outside world.

Modern monks are equally, if not more sheltered than their predecessors. Save for a few phones, a couple of cars, and other basic technology deemed mandatory in the 21st century, the Internet-deprived monks remained consciously ignorant of the current events and political crises that transpired beyond the borders. Libraries also remained free of newspapers, magazines, and any other non-religious or technical literature. In an interview with *60 Minutes*, an Athonite elder from the Simonopetra Monastery claimed that the brothers remained unaware of most, if not all important events, such as 9/11, until several years after the fact. Some today are supposedly still oblivious.

Sketes began to develop in full as the Athonites eased into the idiorrhythmic system, and monks who preferred a more hermetical lifestyle could opt for residence at one of these skete communities. These were not so much complexes as they were cells or "huts" loosely placed around a small central church known as the *"kyriakon."* Such an arrangement was ideal for more introverted souls who desired to be allotted their alone time, yet all the while still maintaining some form of social life through communal worship at the *kyriakon*. As each skete was affiliated to a cenobitic monastery, idiorrhythmic monks relied on the crops or farmland provided to them by the institution for food.

There are a dozen sketes on the peninsula today, the oldest being St. Anne, an affiliate of the Great Lavra. Much like the sketes of the olden days, present communities are overseen by a prior, or a "Fair," an official elected yearly by the elders of the skete.

The New Skete of the Agiou Pavlou monastery

Those who yearned for absolute solitude were directed to the monastic cells sprinkled across the slopes of the Holy Mountain. Cells were individual, often shoddily-built shacks inserted into the nooks and crannies on the face of a cliff. As of 1661, these cell clusters, or hermitages, were obliged by law to associate themselves with a monastery. Similar to skete communities, the affairs of these extreme hermetic compounds were governed by an elder and his spiritual cortége.

The Karoulia Hermitage is by far the most isolated and treacherously situated of all the Athonite hermitages. This is where 10 dauntless hermits reside in single-room huts and claustrophobic caves dangling over the discordant waves on the southwestern cliff face of Mount Athos, described as the "harshest part" of the range.

The first Karoulia hermits certainly took asceticism to an entirely new level. Rarely did these hermits leave their humble abodes, if only because their lone mode of transportation was a rickety pulley system consisting of man-sized baskets and a network of chains and ropes that allowed the monks to haul themselves from one point to the other. Those who were unable to "commute" on their own had to raise a bright flag, thus literally flagging down their neighbors for assistance. The pulley system, as implied by the name of the hermitage – *karoulia* being the Greek word for pulleys – was first perfected by the community on this cliff face.

For food, hermits lowered their baskets to levels populated by cenobitic monks and pilgrims. The baskets were then filled with a loaf of bread, some cheese, or olives. Jugs were used to collect rainwater dripping from nearby cavities.

The burial practice of the Athonite monks is yet another enthralling facet of the culture that developed within the peninsula. To start with, each Athonite monastery was equipped with a charnel house, or a plain vault erected closed to or underneath the *katholikon*. Upon the death of a brother, his corpse was swathed in a *schema* (the ceremonial robes sported by *"schemamonks"*), and his head covered with a *koukoulion*, an elaborate headdress featuring a pill-shaped crown with eared veils that draped over their shoulders. The corpse was then inserted into a cassock – the full-length robes worn by common Athonite monks – which was then sewn shut, acting as a kind of cloth coffin. Last, but not least, a blessed portrait of the Virgin Mary was placed atop the chest of the corpse.

After the funerary service, the cocooned body was transferred to a grave on a small square of cemetery land next to the monastery. Next, the grave was filled and a wooden, "four-pointed cross" was planted onto the freshly-packed earth. The name and date of death of the deceased was then painted onto the cross.

As dictated by tradition, Athonite brotherhoods prayed passionately and without rest for the deceased for a period of no less than 40 days. Day in and day out, the monks fingered the 33 knots on the cables of prayer ropes entangled around their palms, dutifully reciting the appropriate prayers. Monastery cooks also whipped up a platter of *kolivo*, a "memorial dish...[made from] wheat, rye, oat, or rice, as well as honey, raisins, and nuts."

The intensity of the memorial prayers wound down after those 40 days, but for the next three years, the monastery continued to make mention of the deceased at every Liturgy. The memory of the deceased was also immortalized in a safely-kept memorial book known as the "*Kuvaras,*" which contained the names of all the brothers who died since the founding of the institution.

Three years after the monk's passing, his corpse was exhumed from the recycled grave, and experts then stepped forward to inspect the remains. Those with chunks of flesh still clinging to the bones were reburied, while only those that had withered away into bones were collected and prepped for the next stage. Failure to decompose in a timely manner is regarded by superstitious Athonites as proof of the dead's impurity, or lack of discipline in monastic life during his time on Earth. As such, their concerned brothers rolled up their sleeves and reinforced their prayers for him.

Bones of satisfactorily decomposed monks were first rinsed off in concoctions mainly of water and wine before they were transferred to the charnel house. The skulls were, likewise, dried off and transferred to the monastery's ossuary. As this excerpt from *The Catalog of Good Deeds* noted, "[T]he peculiarity of this crypt [lay] in the fact that the deceased, or rather, their remains, are not hidden there, but are in plain sight: the skulls are lined up in rows along the shelves, while the other bones are neatly laid right on the floor along the walls." Some skulls are stacked on top of one another in heaps.

Athonite monasteries also engaged in the tradition of skull-painting. Most complexes, such as the Skete Prophet Elias, opted for the power of simplicity and painted only names and years of birth and death on the foreheads of these skulls. The more artistic Athonites – such as those in the Russian Monastery of Saint Panteleimon, hailed as the "Rembrandts of skull-painting" – used the skulls as canvases for brilliantly-colored works of art.

The Modern Era

"We must always remember that the Lord sees us wrestling with the Enemy, and so we must never be afraid. Even should all hell fall upon us, we must be brave." – St. Silouan the Athonite

The monasteries on the peninsula struggled under the idiorrhythmic system and were beleaguered by mountains of debts between the 15th and 18th centuries. It wasn't until the early 19th century that the Athonites finally climbed out of the holes they had dug themselves. By 1820, most of the monasteries had paid off the bulk of their debts, and local authorities were also in the process of approving the construction of new monasteries, as well as much-needed renovations. As time progressed, more and more monasteries returned to the age-old cenobitic way of life.

Unfortunately, political chaos around the peninsula would strike again shortly after. On the 21st of February in 1821, the Greek War of Independence brought about a spate of Turkish attacks on the Holy Mountain. The peninsula was soon captured by the Ottoman forces, who proceeded to establish a temporary headquarters in Athos, as well as garrisons in several monasteries. The eight-year war was finally concluded in February 1830 with the London Protocol, which officially recognized Greece as an "independent, sovereign state." The last of the Ottomans were only ousted from the mainland in 1912.

For the next 14 years, international councils vigorously deliberated over the peninsula's fate. The first round of discourse was settled with the 1926 Treaty of Lausanne, which placed Athos within the dominion of Greek monarchs, or more specifically, a "self-governing part of the Greek state," thus creating the "Monastic State of Hagion Oros."

For a fleeting moment, peace prevailed, but in 1941, mere months after the Nazis poured into Greece, Mount Athos found itself at the center of a dilemma like no other. In the summer of that fateful year, Professor Franz Dölger arrived at the peninsula and proceeded to carry out a Nazi-themed expedition. Alfred Rosenberg, Reich Minister for the Occupied Eastern Territories, is said to have funded the expedition.

Rosenberg

Dölger's entourage, composed of a mix of intellectuals and military officers, was fully prepared to seize the peninsula by force if necessary, but much to their astonishment, the Athonites appeared to be far more well-disposed to the Germans' unannounced visit. As a matter of fact, they welcomed them with open arms, with a few elders even lauding Hitler as a "great German king who slays the Bolsheviks and the Jews," which they called a "fulfillment of prophecy." Some say the Athonites had no choice but to dance to the tune of the Nazis' fiddle, not to escape what would certainly be their grisly fates, but to ensure the safety of the peninsula's relics. Others claim that the isolated Athonites were unaware of the true depravity of Hitler's crimes. Scott Nevins, author of *The Hitler Icon: How Mount Athos Honored the Führer*, wrote, "In fairness to the residents of Mount Athos, we should note that they had good reason to despise Hitler's nemesis: Communism. Stalin was busy confiscating the Russian Orthodox Church's property and deporting its priests to the gulag, and he had also halted the previously reliable flow of Russian contributions to the monasteries' upkeep."

Whatever the case, the Athonites were keen to avoid the wrath of the Nazis, and the *Iera Espitasia* –a quartet of Athonite elders – took a page from their ancestors' book by penning a tactfully worded letter to the Führer himself. They kindly requested for the dictator to guarantee Mount Athos his personal protection, inflating his ego with the promise of the following title: High Protector of the Holy Mountain. Hitler agreed to this arrangement with great enthusiasm, and as a token of their gratitude, several Athonite monasteries mounted portraits of the dictator on their walls. Some monasteries were even accused of praying for him. Among the accused was the Saint Pantaleimon Monastery, which displayed their Hitler portrait directly below the framed photograph of the ousted Russian Tsar Nicholas II. As scandalized as those outside of the peninsula were about this admittedly serpentine tactic, it worked, because by the end of World War II, Mount Athos remained wholly intact. Conversely, those on the mainland lost 11% of their population, mainly its Jewish residents.

Today, visiting the exclusive peninsula is difficult, but not impossible. An estimated 110 entry visas are supposedly granted each day, consisting of 100 domestic visas and 10 international permits. On account of the number of applicants, pilgrims who wished to plan a trip to the peninsula must apply several months in advance, and owing to the absence of hotels and restaurants in Athos, pilgrims are also expected to book their living quarters with the monasteries themselves. The most commonly granted visa to this "territory within a territory" expire after four days.

Although children as young as 12 are now permitted on Athos (accompanied by an adult), the Byzantine era ban on women and female animals persists. Women have protested against this archaic law, but most have chosen, albeit grudgingly, to respect the prohibition. Other women have willingly trespassed on the property so notoriously off-limits to them, some sparked by defiance and others by the restless spirit of curiosity.

In fact, the first-ever "violation" of the female ban occurred in 1346. The trespasser was Jelen, queen consort of Serbian King Stefan Dušan, who came ashore uninvited. The queen was swiftly intercepted by vigilant monks before she could reach her intended destination, the Serbian Hilander Monastery.

An icon of Jesus in the Hilander Monastery

Mount Athos continued to periodically receive female visitors in the centuries that followed, but interest was inexplicably piqued in the early 1900s, which saw a sudden rash of celibacy-destroying trespassers. In 1929, 26-year-old Maryse Choisy, a disturbed French journalist, allegedly lopped off her own breasts, adopted a male disguise, and lugged her suitcases onto a rented ship, all for the precarious opportunity to experience life amongst the Athonite monks. There, Choisy reportedly remained for an entire month before her true gender was discovered. As soon as the "undercover" journalist returned home, she put pen to pad and documented her tantalizing experiences in a book entitled *A Month With the Men of Mount Athos*. Included in her incredible account were episodes involving a wildly "kinky," yet repentant monk.

Predictably, Choisy's book, branded as an exposé, went to the top of the charts almost at once, but Athonite elders dismissed her tale as no more than tawdry slander. "It is fanciful," reads the official statement released by the Athonites. "[Choisy] probably only saw Mount Athos from a boat. Further, how is it possible for a young and pretty girl, prone to adventures, to remain even a day in whatever type of outfit, amid 5,000 lively, stout monks, and not bring any of them...to temptation? [Could] she have remained unscathed for a month?"

Just three years after Choisy's alleged escapades on Mount Athos, 20-year-old beauty queen and polyglot Aliki Diplarakou, the first Greek contestant to be crowned "Miss Europe" in 1930, made an attempt of her own. As the story goes, Aliki stuffed her hair into her sailor's cap, donned a matching outfit, and crept onto the Athonite shore and into a monastery undetected. Rumor has it that the ravishing brunette caught the eye of a young, attractive monk. She apparently went as so far as to flirt with the unwitting brother, and even managed to snap a photograph of them together. When Aliki was eventually outed and her story was broadcasted by the media, the monk hung up his robes for the last time and left Athos for good. The smitten monk tracked her down with a ring in his pocket, only to discover that Aliki was already happily married. Devastated, the monk spiraled into a horrid depression and was ultimately driven mad by his heartbreak, spending the rest of his miserable days in a psychiatric facility.

The last straw would come in the spring of 1953. On the 17th of April, a 22-year-old woman named Maria Poimenidou adopted a male disguise and conned her way into a monastery, where she enjoyed the company of Athonite monks for two days. Understandably, Maria's visit prompted a furor on the peninsula, which led to the passing of "Legislative Decree 2623/1953." As stated by the decree, any woman who dared to set foot on Athos from that point forward would be subject to a maximum penalty of 12 months behind bars.

The only woman who has managed to obtain an invite was Eliza Charlotte Alexander, the second wife of Statford Canning, British ambassador to the Ottoman Empire, but even then, the Athonites made clear that such an invite was most likely a one-time phenomenon. As Patriarch Anthimos put it, the Athonites "understood the reasons for the visit, [but] he strictly recommended not repeating it."

Unyielding as the Athonites were about upholding the ban on women, they were known to show compassion to their neighbors during dire times. Mount Athos served as a hideout for women and children refugees twice, once in the Greek War of Independence, and again during the three-year Greek Civil War of 1946.

The peninsula's prohibition on women is just one of the controversies clinging to the Athonites' reputation. An article from the April 1941 issue of *Time Magazine* highlighted some of the other supposed debauchery that the Athonites engaged in. "[An] alarming number of [Athonite] monks have taken to smoking, alcohol, [and] even narcotics," the article exclaimed. "And the immemorial escape from celibacy has threatened to become a fever sickening the whole 'Great Academy of the Greek Clergy.' The Greek press has stormed about the kidnapping of male children for the monks of Athos, and motorboats carrying male prostitutes are constantly reported chugging into the monastery harbors."

Athonites have also been maligned by critics for their views on certain human rights issues, especially within the LGBT community. In a shocking interview entitled "They Take Psychotropic Drugs on Mount Athos," published by the "E" (Εψιλον) magazine in April 2001, a former Athonite monk by the name of Michael Haztiantoniou vilified the monks for a number of hypocrisies, including their treatment of homosexual monks. According to Brother Michael, who lived on Athos between 1973 and 1988, an Athonite monk from a nearby monastery suddenly died of an unspecified illness. When authorities discovered that the deceased was gay, they immediately decided to wash their hands clean of him, refusing him the honor of burying him alongside his fellow monks. His name was also omitted from the *Kuvaras*.

The Athonites have also been criticized for their active campaign against transgender individuals in recent years, branding it "gender dysphoria" and a Satan-given "mental illness." This was their response to a 2017 law that enabled Greek citizens over the age of 15 to alter the genders on their national identity cards without proof of a sex-change operation: "It is another violation of God's law, just like existing legislation which permits cohabitation agreements between same-sex couples. If we do not resist, then our ancestors will rise from their graves." In the same breath, they argued that transgender men, whom they regarded as "women," could now visit Mount Athos as they pleased without suffering any legal repercussions.

Today, many blame the irresistibly seductive powers of 21st century technology, amongst other factors, for the dramatic decrease in the peninsula's population. In 1905, official records indicate that there were 7,553 monks on Mount Athos, and the ethnicities of the Athonite residents were "3,207 Greeks, 3,615 Russians, 340 Bulgarians, 288 Romanians, 53 Georgians, 18 Servians, and 32 belonging to other nationalities." There were 21 principal monasteries, listed according to their place on the hierarchy: "The Great Lavra, Iviron, Vatopedi, Chilandarion, St. Dionysus, Coutloumousi, Pantocrator, Xiropatamos, Zograf, Docheiarion, Caracalla, Philotheos, Simopetra, St. Paul, Stauroniceta, Xenophon, Osiou Gregoriou, Esphigmenon, St. Panteleimon, St. Anna, and finally the Monastery of Karyses."

Recently, the first road was built on Mount Athos, courtesy of Greek authorities, but such things could do nothing to heal the deteriorating morale and increasing differences widening the rift between the Athonite brothers. The once-coveted peninsula's loss in appeal was undeniable, as the 40,000 monks who once lived there during its height in the 1300s had dwindled away to 7,500 by the 20th century. Numbers continued to plunge, and today, only about 1,500 monks remain.

Meteora in the Modern Era

"Nothing can be more strange and wonderful than this romantic region, which is unlike anything I have ever seen before or since. In...any other mountainous region where I have been, there is nothing at all to be compared to these extraordinary peaks..." – Robert Curzon, English traveler on the Meteoran Pillars, 1849

Apart from the mysterious monasteries of Meteora, part of its charm lies in the compelling legends and delightful miracles associated with the city of stone. One of the most titillating tales is about the Dragon of Varlaam. Once upon a time, a colossal, scaly beast, which supposedly dwelled in the massive cave underneath the Monastery of Varlaam, viciously hounded the villagers for decades on end. The residents and livestock of the neighboring village, Kastraki, suffered the worst of the assaults. The villagers promptly retired to their homes and shepherded their livestock into their barns at dusk, bolting every last door shut, but the cunning dragon continued to feed by smashing its way into farms and homes and swooping down upon unsuspecting children and barnyard animals.

Unable to fend off the beast on their own, a band of villagers climbed up to the Monastery of Varlaam and enlisted the help of its monks. Together, the villagers and brothers of Varlaam brainstormed and employed various tactics to frighten off the notorious dragon, all to no avail. Finally, a selfless brother stepped forth, submitting himself as a sacrifice. Late that evening, the stoic monk walked to the end of the rock column, thunderously invoking a curse against the dragon before diving off the edge of the formation. Suddenly, the ground began to tremble violently, causing the ceiling of the dragon's cave to disintegrate and killing the savage beast. Thanks to the story, this cave, which can still be seen today, is known as the "*Drakospilia*," or the "Dragon's Cave."

A lighter tale often repeated by the locals is about an unnamed 15th century Meteoran monastery. One fateful morning, which began like any other morning, the monks filed into their *katholikon* and attended the long liturgical service. Following the service, the brothers headed back to their cells for a quick rest, only to find the doors boarded shut. The monks sternly rapped on the doors with their knuckles, demanding that the squatters vacate their cells immediately. To their dismay, the enormous family of mostly boisterous young boys who had captured this wing of the monastery spilled out without warning, swinging their swords, bludgeons, and weapons as they chased off the monks. The family, if the story is to be believed, did not budge from the premises for a staggering 87 years. The monks eventually succeeded in getting back their cells, though how they did so remains unclear.

Meteora, as one might expect, is also an endless source of inexplicable, but joyous miracles. Once such miracle is said to have transpired in St. George Mantilas, one of the most popular hermitages in Meteora. One year in the spring of the 17th century, an esteemed Muslim proprietor snuck into the "sacred forest" of St. George and began hacking down one of the hallowed trees. In the midst of the desecration, however, the man's axe suddenly slipped from his grasp, and the confused man crumpled to the floor, howling in pain as he clutched his paralyzed hand and arm, apparently immobilized and inflamed by the guardian spirit of St. George himself. His withering cries of pain soon attracted a crowd, including his tearful wife. The man was examined by several physicians, but they could not reach a proper diagnosis. Fresh out of scientific options, the man's wife, acting upon the advice of an Islamic sage, presented to her ailing husband the most precious of gifts in the local Muslim tradition, her most prized silk veil. Miraculously, the paralysis in the man's arm was instantly lifted, fully restored to its former glory.

In honor of the miraculous cure, which the locals have attributed to St. George, a single rope, attached to a pair of trees like a clothesline, was installed by the entrance of the Cave of Agios Georgios Mantilas, or in English, the "Cave of St. George with the Scarves." Tied to the rope is a flapping row of scarves in a rainbow of bright colors, and from a distance, the scarves resemble a flock of colorful birds. These scarves are replaced every year in a climbing competition, a sport engaged in by the "Mandilarades" (or Mantilarades), a name given to the young men (and occasionally women) who volunteer to retrieve the old scarves and lace up the new *mandiles*, or "headscarves." Typically, the climbers were allowed to keep the old scarves as mementos, one that apparently guaranteed them a lifetime of good health. The new scarves, insist his believers, ensure that the blessings St. George showered upon them regarding clean bills of health, lasting and fulfilling marriages, and other good fortunes continued.

The Meteoran monks accomplished far more than what is often touted. On top of their outstanding architectural skills and their irreplaceable treasuries, numerous Meteoran monks from well-to-do backgrounds funded the establishment of several ecclesiastical schools and learning centers out of their own pockets. The most prestigious of all these institutions is undoubtedly the Academy of Meteora, founded by Socration halfway into the 1500s.

Another was the Academy of Aghios Stephanos, which was attended by a slew of brilliant scholars, among them 19th century Orthodox Bishop Dorotheos Scholarios. The same alumnus went on to establish the Dorothean School in the Thessalian city of Trikala. Other monks of privileged status contributed to the flourishing Meteoran enlightenment by donating rare books, manuscripts, and other literary treasures to the monasteries' libraries. The magnanimous Paision Klinovitis, Bishop of Stagon, gifted to the Monastery of Aghios Stephanos not just a few books, but his entirely personal collection. The monks' mission to enhance the theological knowledge of Meteora reached its height in 1845, when a trio of *protas* from three Meteoran monasteries – Friars Meteora, Varlaam, and Stephanos – wrote a letter pledging 500 *grosia* (a type of Greek currency) to all the holy schools in Trikki, which was to go towards the teachers' salaries. Friar Konstantios of the Monastery of Aghios Stephanos, who established the Konstantion Academy of Kalambaka in Meteora, was another well-known patron of Trikalan institutions.

Between the late 17th and early 19th centuries, explorers and travelers from both near and far flocked to Meteora, which had become a landmark in its own right. Among this lengthy list of visitors were Sweden-born J. Bjornstahl, who visited the city of stone in 1779, the British Lord R. Curzon in 1834, French archaeologist L. Heuzey in 1858, and Dean Uspenkij from Russia in 1859. These travelers, who recorded their experiences in their journals, are credited with much of the knowledge that the outside world has of Meteora today. Having said that, Meteoran monks have accused many of these "biased" travelers with propagating inaccurate factoids and "show[ing] no sympathy and no understanding of the Orthodox monasticism."

Even as people began to show renewed interest in Meteora, it was during this period of time that the Meteoran monks began to part ways with the heavenly columns. The defenses provided by the height and inaccessibility of these pillars, which St. Athanasios the Meteorite hoped would persist, was no longer impenetrable by the time of Turkish rule. For these reasons, the monks fled, albeit with heavy hearts.

As it turned out, it was just as well, for the worst of the assaults was yet to come. In 1809, a stouthearted rebel priest named Thimios Vlahavas raised a fierce revolution against the Turkish rulers, and in retaliation, armies commanded by Ali Pasa of Ioannina seized the Holy Monastery of Saint Demetrius of Meteora, also known as the "Holy Lavra of Thessaly," said to be the base of Vlahavas's revolutionary campaign. Shortly thereafter, the Turks ordered the immediate shutdown of all monasteries in Thessaly, including those in Meteora. Finally, they took all the abbots of Ioannina hostage, imprisoning them for several years. Vlahavas was barbarically quartered.

During the 1700s and the 1800s, the Meteoran monasteries also served as hideouts for patriotic souls involved in the Greek independence movement, and more wounds were inflicted upon the Meteoran monasteries in the 20th century. During World War II, multiple bombs rained down on the area, which blasted multiple monasteries into rubble. To make matters worse, German and Italian soldiers, as well as local thieves, plundered a number of the monasteries, and their efforts were made easier by the installation of the staircases about two decades prior.

Meteora was struck by another spate of attacks during the Greek Civil War, which lasted from 1946-1949. In addition to the injuries inflicted by those who had converted the monasteries into shelters and military nerve centers, they were battered again by more German mortars. The "hagiographied dome of the Almighty and the Four Evangelists," belonging to the Chapel of St. Charalambos in the Monastery of Aghios Stephanos, was nearly damaged beyond repair, and the original Church of Aghios Stephanos was also the target of a terrible looting spree. The faces and the eyes of the saints in the frescoes were either defaced with writing or scrubbed off.

As Meteora's population plummeted, an entirely new group of people began to move in to the doomed city of stone. Like Mount Athos, which continues to uphold its strictly all-male policy to this day, women were banned from setting foot on Meteora until the first decades of the 1900s.

Why the Meteoran authorities had this change of heart is still a matter of dispute. Some say that a frightful fire erupted on one of the monasteries in the fall of 1920, and when they heard the monks' cries of distress, a brave group consisting of only village women scurried up the newly built stairs and extinguished the crackling flames. To express their gratitude, Meteoran authorities elected to annul the antiquated law and began to welcome pious women (nuns) into their land. Meteora received its first official laywoman visitor in 1921, when it was graced with the presence of Queen Marie of Romania. Ivana Greslikova, author of "Meteora, Greece: A Spiritual and Natural Wonder of the World," explained, "The monks had to make a decision whether to break the rule and accept the help from nuns (this was not acceptable because of their [vow of celibacy]) or...to let the monastic community die. Their community survived – so [it can be supposed that] an exception was made eventually..." Today, cenobitic nuns can be found in the Monasteries of Aghios Stephanos and Roussanos.

In spite of the centuries of history that took place within the hallowed region, this unique network of monastic complexes did not receive the recognition it was certainly due until the late 20th century. The monastic state of Meteora is now classified as a "protected monument" of the UNESCO World Heritage Site, and in 1995 it was declared a "holy land [that is] unchangeable and inviolable."

Owing to the endless technological advances and the excitement of city life in the 21st century, the population of Meteora is as scarce as ever. As one Meteoran brother lamented, "Look at us now! Ah...the young don't want us anymore!" Today, only 6 of the 24 monasteries remain, and even those – the Great Meteoron, as well as the Monasteries of Varlaam, Roussanou, the Holy Trinity, the Aghios Nikolas, and the Aghios Stephanos – are inhabited by no more than 15 monks and 16 nuns.

Nevertheless, Meteora remains a popular tourist attraction, with more than 600,000 pilgrims and visitors each year.

Aghios Nikolas

Aghios Stephanos

Vaggelis Vlahos' picture of the Roussanou Monastery

Online Resources

Other books about Greece by Charles River Editors

Other books about Mount Athos on Amazon

Other books about Meteora on Amazon

Meteora Bibliography

Robbins, L. *22 Facts That Will Make You Want to Visit the Meteora Monasteries in Greece*. 15 Feb. 2016, monkeysandmountains.com/meteora-monasteries/. Accessed 12 July 2018.

Editors, M E. *10 Fascinating Facts About Meteora, Greece*. 24 Feb. 2015, medexperience.com/blog/10-fascinating-facts-about-meteora-in-greece/. Accessed 12 July 2018.

Editors, J F. *Interesting Facts about Meteora*. 2015, justfunfacts.com/interesting-facts-about-meteora/. Accessed 12 July 2018.

Editors, T T. *7 Interesting Facts about Meteora Greece*. 2018, www.traveladvisortips.com/7-interesting-facts-about-meteora-greece/. Accessed 12 July 2018.

Nikolaoy, K. *THE METEORA MONASTERIES*. 2015, www.visitmeteora.travel/the-meteora-monasteries/. Accessed 12 July 2018.

Dilouambaka, E. *The Story Behind The Mountain-Top Monasteries of Meteora, Greece*. 20 Oct. 2016, theculturetrip.com/europe/greece/articles/the-story-behind-the-mountain-top-monasteries-of-meteora-greece/. Accessed 12 July 2018.

Alexander, R. *The Magical Monasteries Of Meteora*. 4 Nov. 2014, www.journeywonders.com/the-magical-monasteries-of-meteora/. Accessed 12 July 2018.

Andreev, A. *METEORA IN GREECE – FAITH ON THE TOP OF THE WORLD*. 2017, www.andrey-andreev.com/en/meteora-greece/. Accessed 12 July 2018.

Greslikova, I. *METEORA, GREECE: A SPIRITUAL AND NATURAL WONDER OF THE WORLD*. 4 Aug. 2015, nomadisbeautiful.com/travel-blogs/meteora-greece-spiritual-natural-wonder-of-the-world/. Accessed 12 July 2018.

Editors, J N. *Meteora – an Unusual Place in Greece Where Monks Love Extreme Sports!* 18 Feb. 2016, www.journalofnomads.com/meteora-unusual-place-greece-monks-love-extreme-sports/. Accessed 12 July 2018.

Editors, M G. *The Promised Land: Spiritual Majesty Above the Clouds*. 2017, www.mysteriousgreece.com/travel-guides/mainland/thessaly/meteora/. Accessed 12 July 2018.

Editors, G. *Meteora History*. 2015, www.greeka.com/thessaly/meteora/meteora-history.htm. Accessed 12 July 2018.

Editors, K. *History of Meteora*. 2018, www.kalampaka.com/en/meteora/history/. Accessed 12 July 2018.

Nikolaoy, K. *THE UNKNOWN MINYANS: THE HIDDEN HISTORY BEHIND THE LEGENDS AND MYTHS (PART 1)*. 2017, www.visitmeteora.travel/the-unknown-minyans-the-hidden-history-behind-the-legends-and-myths-part-1/. Accessed 12 July 2018.

Nikolaoy, K. *THE UNKNOWN MINYANS: THE HIDDEN HISTORY BEHIND THE LEGENDS AND MYTHS (PART 2)*. 2017, www.visitmeteora.travel/the-unknown-minyans-the-hidden-history-behind-the-legends-and-myths-part-2/. Accessed 12 July 2018.

Sanidopoulos, J. *Meteora's Prison for Monks*. 28 Aug. 2012, www.johnsanidopoulos.com/2012/08/meteoras-prison-for-monks.html. Accessed 12 July 2018.

Editors, B R. *Meteora: to the Heights, a Pain in the Neck and Views from Prison*. 14 May 2012, barrysramblings.com/2012/05/14/meteora-to-the-heights-and-views-from-prison/. Accessed 12 July 2018.

Editors, A O. *Meteora: the Impressive Greek Monasteries Suspended in the Air*. 2 Aug. 2015, www.ancient-origins.net/ancient-places-europe/meteora-impressive-greek-monasteries-suspended-air-003530. Accessed 12 July 2018.

Editors, V M. *Meteora and Its People*. 6 Apr. 2013, visitmeteora.wordpress.com/tag/mythology/. Accessed 12 July 2018.

Willson, L. *Meteora*. 2014, www.meteora-greece.info/Links/Meteora-Poem.htm. Accessed 12 July 2018.

Editors, A O. *The Legendary Tower of Babel*. 23 Apr. 2014, www.ancient-origins.net/myths-legends/tower-babel-001583. Accessed 12 July 2018.

Editors, B S. *The Tower of Babel - Bible Story*. 2 Nov. 2016, www.biblestudytools.com/bible-stories/the-tower-of-babel.html. Accessed 12 July 2018.

Isaacs, J. *The Tower Of Babel*. 22 Feb. 2018, www.chabad.org/library/article_cdo/aid/246611/jewish/The-Tower-Of-Babel.htm. Accessed 12 July 2018.

Fairchild, M. *Lesson From the Tower of Babel Bible Story*. 13 Dec. 2017, www.thoughtco.com/the-tower-of-babel-700219. Accessed 12 July 2018.

Editors, M T. *METEORA : THE CREATION OF A UNIQUE GEOLOGICAL PHENOMENON*. 23 Nov. 2017, meteora.com/meteora-creation-unique-geological-phenomenon/. Accessed 12 July 2018.

Editors, I M. *Natural Environment-Geology*. 2017, www.infotouristmeteora.gr/main-menu/meteora/natural-environment-geology/. Accessed 12 July 2018.

Editors, I M. *The Monasticism at the Holy Meteora and Its Living Witness over the Centuries*. 2017, www.infotouristmeteora.gr/main-menu/meteora/monasticism-in-meteora/. Accessed 12 July 2018.

Editors, G C. *Fingers of Giants - Meteora Earthcache*. 14 Sept. 2010, www.geocaching.com/geocache/GC2F643_fingers-of-giants-meteora-earthcache?guid=a3feffb7-adc8-430c-818c-5d8d225ea7f0. Accessed 12 July 2018.

Editors, W O. *Meteora—Towering Rock Pillars*. 2001, wol.jw.org/en/wol/d/r1/lp-e/102001605. Accessed 12 July 2018.

Editors, A. *Meteora - Climbing in Unusual Rock Geology*. 27 Sept. 2016, www.alaturka.info/en/greece/trikala/3457-meteora-climbing-in-unusual-rock-geology. Accessed 12 July 2018.

Kokoni, D. *Meteora: The Ever-Shining Lighthouse of Orthodoxy*. 2017, users.sch.gr/elianos/meteora_in_eng.htm. Accessed 13 July 2018.

Nikolaoy, K. *THE LEGEND OF THE DRAGON'S CAVE*. 2017, www.visitmeteora.travel/the-legend-of-the-dragons-cave/. Accessed 13 July 2018.

Nikolaoy, K. *RUINS AND HIDDEN GEMS*. 2017, www.visitmeteora.travel/ruins-hidden-gems-2/. Accessed 13 July 2018.

Editors, A H. *Meteora Monasteries*. 2015, www.hotelalexiou.com/en/meteora-monasteries-kalabaka/. Accessed 13 July 2018.

Editors, M G. *Abbeys - Monasteries*. 2014, www.mygreece.travel/en/things-to-see-and-do/religion/abbeys-monasteries/meteora.php. Accessed 13 July 2018.

Banquet, B. *FIRST MONKS AND SUNSETS*. 29 Sept. 2014, clangstonadventuretime.wordpress.com/2014/09/29/first-monks-and-sunsets/. Accessed 13 July 2018.

Boutsia, C. *Dererted Monasteries - Hermitages*. 2017, users.sch.gr/elianos/meteora_askitiria_eng.htm. Accessed 13 July 2018.

Editors, V T. *Meteora*. 2014, volostaxiservice.com/Meteora.html. Accessed 13 July 2018.

Sophianos, D Z. *A Brief History of the Monastic Community of Meteora*. 3 Oct. 2014, meteoronlithopolis.gr/en/23-history/83. Accessed 13 July 2018.

Editors, I M. *The First Cave-Dwelling Ascetics*. 2015, www.infotouristmeteora.gr/main-menu/meteora/sketes-hermitages-dependencies/. Accessed 13 July 2018.

Nikolaoy, K. *DOUPIANI HERMITAGE*. 2017, www.visitmeteora.travel/doupiani-hermitage/. Accessed 13 July 2018.

Editors, T B. *The Battle of the Titans*. 2017, www.talesbeyondbelief.com/titans-mythology/battle-of-the-titans.htm. Accessed 13 July 2018.

Editors, G G. *Titanomachy*. 9 Feb. 2017, greekgodsandgoddesses.net/myths/titanomachy/. Accessed 13 July 2018.

Editors, G M. *Cyclopes*. 2016, www.greekmythology.com/Myths/Creatures/Cyclopes/cyclopes.html. Accessed 13 July 2018.

Editors, G. *Cyclopean Walls Source: Www.greeka.com*. 2014, www.greeka.com/peloponnese/mycenae/mycenae-excursions/mycenae-cyclopean-walls.htm. Accessed 13 July 2018.

Nikolaoy, K. *THE BYZANTINE CHURCH OF VIRGIN MARY*. 2015, www.visitmeteora.travel/the-byzantine-church-of-virgin-mary/. Accessed 16 July 2018.

Editors, E T. *Wildlife/ Fauna in Trikala*. 2018, www.ecotourism-greece.com/tourism/activity/wildlife-tours-greece/trikala. Accessed 16 July 2018.

Nikolaoy, K. *CLIMATE – VEGETATION – FAUNA*. 2018, www.visitmeteora.travel/climate-vegetation-fauna/. Accessed 16 July 2018.

Editors, H W. *Weather in Meteora*. 2017, www.holiday-weather.com/meteora/. Accessed 16 July 2018.

Lovgren, S. *Is Troy True? The Evidence Behind Movie Myth*. 14 May 2004, news.nationalgeographic.com/news/2004/05/did-troy-exist-evidence-behind-movie-myth/. Accessed 16 July 2018.

Jarus, O. *Ancient Troy: The City & the Legend.* 25 Aug. 2017, www.livescience.com/38191-ancient-troy.html. Accessed 16 July 2018.

Editors, A G. *Ancient Greece Reloaded.* 2018, www.ancientgreecereloaded.com/files/ancient_greece_reloaded_website/archaeological_sites_and_temples/sites_meteora.php. Accessed 16 July 2018.

Editors, M F. *ANCIENT GREEK RELIGION, RITUALS AND WORSHIP.* 2015, mythologyfacts.weebly.com/religion-rituals-and-worship.html. Accessed 16 July 2018.

Lambert, T. *Http://Www.localhistories.org/Monasteries.html.* 2011, www.localhistories.org/monasteries.html. Accessed 16 July 2018.

Editors, J V. *Jews in Islamic Countries: The Treatment of Jews.* Sept. 2011, www.jewishvirtuallibrary.org/the-treatment-of-jews-in-arab-islamic-countries. Accessed 16 July 2018.

Editors, R. *Christianity in the Ottoman Empire.* 20 July 2017, www.revolvy.com/page/Christianity-in-the-Ottoman-Empire. Accessed 16 July 2018.

Editors, G O. *History: The Great Epochs of Orthodoxy.* 2018, www.kimisis.org/our-faith/history-of-orthodox. Accessed 16 July 2018.

Editors, H W. *HISTORY OF CHRISTIANITY .* 2013, www.historyworld.net/wrldhis/PlainTextHistories.asp?ParagraphID=dmc#1136. Accessed 23 July 2018.

Editors, E N. *What Is the Difference between the Orthodox and Catholic Churches?* 25 Nov. 2016, www.euronews.com/2016/11/25/catholic-and-orthodox-christian-churches-compared. Accessed 23 July 2018.

Meyendorff, J. *Eastern Orthodoxy.* 28 Feb. 2018, www.britannica.com/topic/Eastern-Orthodoxy. Accessed 23 July 2018.

Editors, O W. *Symeon the New Theologian.* 10 Feb. 2016, orthodoxwiki.org/Symeon_the_New_Theologian. Accessed 23 July 2018.

Editors, C O. *Monastery of the Transfiguration of Christ Highest, Largest of Six Monasteries of Meteora.* 23 Mar. 2012, www.catholic.org/travel/story.php?id=45386. Accessed 23 July 2018.

Nikolaoy, K. *ST. NICHOLAS (BADOVAS).* 2014, www.visitmeteora.travel/st-nicholas-badovas/. Accessed 23 July 2018.

Editors, C I. *Meteora*. 2016, cromwell-intl.com/travel/greece/meteora.html. Accessed 23 July 2018.

Editors, K. *Holy Church of the Dormition of Theotokos*. 2018, www.kalampaka.com/en/kalampaka/holy-church-dormition-of-theotokos/. Accessed 23 July 2018.

Editors, W C. *Andronicus III Palaeologus Emperor of the East 1296-1341*. 2010, worldcat.org/identities/lccn-n85041125/. Accessed 24 July 2018.

Editors, I H. *Meteora, Greece's City in the Sky*. 24 Nov. 2013, i-love-hellas.blogspot.com/2013/11/meteora-greeces-city-in-sky.html. Accessed 24 July 2018.

Editors, O I. *Christianity and the Ottoman Empire*. 2017, www.oxfordislamicstudies.com/article/opr/t253/e2. Accessed 24 July 2018.

Editors, H G. *The Ottoman Period*. 2009, www.ahistoryofgreece.com/turkish.htm. Accessed 24 July 2018.

Editors, M H. *Athos in the 11th–15th Centuries*. 2018, www.macedonian-heritage.gr/Athos/General/History.html#Anchor-Athos-47383. Accessed 24 July 2018.

Editors, M K. *History of Macedonia 1354-1833*. 2017, macedonia.kroraina.com/en/av/av_6_1.htm. Accessed 24 July 2018.

Editors, O C. *Venerable Dionysius of Olympus*. 24 Jan. 2008, oca.org/saints/lives/2008/01/24/100295-venerable-dionysius-of-olympus. Accessed 24 July 2018.

Editors, O W. *Https://Orthodoxwiki.org/Meteora*. 19 Apr. 2017, orthodoxwiki.org/Meteora. Accessed 24 July 2018.

Boutsia, C. *The Holy Monastery of the Great Meteoron*. 2014, users.sch.gr/elianos/meteora_megalo_meteoro_eng.htm. Accessed 24 July 2018.

Editors, N P. *Meteora Monasteries: The Great Meteoron*. 11 Nov. 2010, narrowpathways.blogspot.com/2010/11/meteora-monasteries-great-meteoron.html. Accessed 24 July 2018.

Editors, S D. *Great Meteoron Monastery, Meteora*. 2012, www.sacred-destinations.com/greece/meteora-great-meteoron-monastery. Accessed 24 July 2018.

Blazeki, G. *"Suspended in the Air"- the Breathtaking Monasteries of Meteora*. 22 Dec. 2016, www.thevintagenews.com/2016/12/22/suspended-in-the-air-the-breathtaking-monasteries-of-meteora/. Accessed 24 July 2018.

Nikolaoy, K. *HOLY TRINITY MONASTERY*. 2017, www.visitmeteora.travel/holy-trinity-monastery/. Accessed 24 July 2018.

Editors, O W. *Pantocrator*. 15 Jan. 2013, orthodoxwiki.org/Pantocrator. Accessed 24 July 2018.

Facorellis, Y. *The Cave of Theopetra, Kalambaka: Radiocarbon Evidence for 50,000 Years of Human Presence*. 18 July 2016, www.cambridge.org/core/journals/radiocarbon/article/div-classtitlethe-cave-of-theopetra-kalambaka-radiocarbon-evidence-for-50000-years-of-human-presencediv/DB281418EA9F6ECD018C0540C80514B2. Accessed 24 July 2018.

Editors, W C. *0466 GREECE (Thessaly) - Meteora (UNESCO WHS)*. 13 Jan. 2013, worldcometomyhome.blogspot.com/2013/01/0466-greece-meteora-in-heavens-above.html. Accessed 24 July 2018.

Sanidopoulos, J. *Saint Nektarios and Theophanes, Founders of Barlaam Monastery at Meteora*. 17 May 2017, www.johnsanidopoulos.com/2017/05/saints-nektarios-and-theophanes.html. Accessed 24 July 2018.

Editors, G A. *Greece Travel: Meteora Monasteries Page 4*. 2015, www.greeceathensaegeaninfo.com/destinations_greece_meteora_kalambaka4.htm. Accessed 24 July 2018.

Editors, R M. *Meteora and Pelion*. 2016, www.route4u.net/meteora.htm. Accessed 24 July 2018.

Editors, O W. *Schemamonk*. 10 June 2008, orthodoxwiki.org/Schemamonk. Accessed 24 July 2018.

Alavanou, E. *Meteora: Monasteries on the Edge*. 12 Dec. 2016, www.greece-is.com/meteora-monasteries-on-the-edge/. Accessed 24 July 2018.

Nikolaoy, K. *ST. GEORGE MADILAS*. 2018, www.visitmeteora.travel/st-george-madilas/. Accessed 24 July 2018.

Nikolaoy, K. *ST GEORGE THE MANDILAS, THE ORIGINS OF A 300 YEARS OLD METEORA TRADITION*. 2017, www.visitmeteora.travel/st-george-the-mandilas-the-origins-of-a-300-years-old-meteora-tradition/. Accessed 24 July 2018.

Editors, L N. *Meteora – Greece, A Magical Image of a Fairytale*. 13 Jan. 2011, livenowtravel.wordpress.com/2011/01/13/meteora-greece-a-magical-image-of-a-fairytale/. Accessed 24 July 2018.

Editors, S D. *Agios Stefanos Monastery, Meteora*. 2015, www.sacred-destinations.com/greece/meteora-agios-stefanos-monastery. Accessed 24 July 2018.

Editors, K. *Holy Monastery of Saint Stephen*. 2017, www.kalampaka.com/en/meteora-monasteries/monastery-of-saint-stephen/. Accessed 24 July 2018.

Elytes, O. (2004). *The Collected Poems of Odysseus Elytis*. JHU Press.

Papademetriou, T. (2015). *Render unto the Sultan: Power, Authority, and the Greek Orthodox Church in the Early Ottoman Centuries*. OUP Oxford.

Nichol, D. M. (1993). *The Last Centuries of Byzantium, 1261-1453*. Cambridge University Press.

Mount Athos Bibliography

Editors, B. *Why Are Women Banned from Mount Athos?* 27 May 2016, www.bbc.com/news/magazine-36378690. Accessed 4 July 2018.

Editors, S L. *The Land and Its People*. 2015, sacredland.org/mount-athos-greece/. Accessed 4 July 2018.

Editors, V M. *Mount Athos Chronology*. 2015, www.visitmountathos.eu/chronology.html. Accessed 4 July 2018.

Editors, M H. *The History of Mount Athos*. 2017, www.macedonian-heritage.gr/Athos/General/History.html. Accessed 4 July 2018.

Editors, S D. *Mount Athos, Greece*. 2013, www.sacred-destinations.com/greece/mt-athos. Accessed 4 July 2018.

Editors, O. *Facts about Mount Athos You Should Know*. 21 June 2018, ouranoupoli.gr/facts-about-mount-athos-you-should-know/. Accessed 4 July 2018.

Nevins, S. *A Short History of Women Who Have Entered Mount Athos [Updated]*. 31 Jan. 2015, scottnevinssuicide.wordpress.com/2015/01/31/a-short-history-of-women-who-have-entered-mount-athos/. Accessed 4 July 2018.

Sanidopoulos, J. *Women Who Violated the Avaton of Mount Athos*. 4 Aug. 2014, www.johnsanidopoulos.com/2014/08/women-who-violated-avaton-of-mount-athos.html. Accessed 4 July 2018.

Squires, N. *Monks of Mt Athos Fear New Gender Law Could Enable Women into Their All-Male Sanctuary*. 17 Oct. 2017, www.telegraph.co.uk/news/2017/10/17/monks-mt-athos-fear-new-gender-law-could-enable-women-all-male/. Accessed 4 July 2018.

Grohmann, K. *Greek Women Enter Male-Only Mount Athos Community*. 9 Jan. 2008, www.reuters.com/article/us-greece-women-athos/greek-women-enter-male-only-mount-athos-community-idUSL0945881020080109. Accessed 4 July 2018.

Nevins, S. *The Hitler Icon: How Mount Athos Honored the Führer*. 21 Feb. 2016, scottnevinssuicide.wordpress.com/2016/02/21/the-hitler-icon-how-mount-athos-honored-the-fuhrer/. Accessed 4 July 2018.

Nevins, S. *Mount Athos, Homosexuality, Addiction to Heavy Psychotropic Drugs & Suicide (Monk Michael, 2001)*. 26 Jan. 2016, scottnevinssuicide.wordpress.com/2016/01/26/mount-athos-homosexuality-addiction-to-heavy-psychotropic-drugs-έψιλον-τεύχος-524/. Accessed 4 July 2018.

Editors, O C. *26 Martyrs of the Zographou Monastery on Mt. Athos at the Hands of the Crusaders*. 10 Oct. 2013, oca.org/saints/lives/2013/10/10/108024-26-martyrs-of-the-zographou-monastery-on-mt-athos-at-the-hands-o. Accessed 4 July 2018.

Orthodox Christian Quotes. Edited by S Mojsovki and K Wilkerson, 1 Nov. 2007, theodorakis.net/orthodoxquotescomplete.html. Accessed 4 July 2018.

Findler, R, and M Fidler. *The Holy Mountain: Monks of Mount Athos – Photo Essay*. 5 Jan. 2017, www.theguardian.com/artanddesign/2017/jan/05/the-holy-mountain-monks-of-mount-athos-photo-essay. Accessed 4 July 2018.

Gray, M. *Mount Athos*. 2017, sacredsites.com/europe/greece/mount_athos.html. Accessed 4 July 2018.

Editors, M. *A History of Mount Athos*. 2017, www.monachos.net/library/index.php/monasticism/athos/113-a-history-of-mount-athos. Accessed 4 July 2018.

Editors, C P. *The History Of Mount Athos*. 2018, www.christian-pilgrimage-journeys.com/mount-athos/history-mount-athos/. Accessed 4 July 2018.

Editors, C P. *The History Of Mount Athos (4th Century - 14th Century)*. 2017, www.christian-pilgrimage-journeys.com/mount-athos/4thcentury-14thcentury/. Accessed 4 July 2018.

Dilouambaka, E. *A Brief History Of Mount Athos*. 28 Oct. 2016, theculturetrip.com/europe/greece/articles/a-brief-history-of-mount-athos/. Accessed 4 July 2018.

Roten, J G. *Mount Athos and Mary*. 2017, udayton.edu/imri/mary/m/mount-athos-and-mary.php. Accessed 5 July 2018.

Editors, O C. *No Girls Allowed – The Greek State That Forbids Both Human and Animal Females*. 23 Jan. 2015, www.odditycentral.com/travel/no-girls-allowed-the-greek-state-that-forbids-both-human-and-animal-females.html. Accessed 5 July 2018.

Editors, V. *Mount Athos in Greece Forbids Women from Entering Because of a Religious Reason (11 Pics)*. 23 June 2016, www.vorply.com/world/list/find-out-why-mount-athos-in-greece-is-forbidden-for-women/. Accessed 5 July 2018.

Foster, D. *One Small Step for Womankind in an All-Male Greek State*. 18 Sept. 2012, www.theguardian.com/commentisfree/belief/2012/sep/18/mount-athos-male-greek-state. Accessed 5 July 2018.

Editors, H C. *BYZANTINE EMPIRE*. 2017, www.history.com/topics/ancient-history/byzantine-empire. Accessed 5 July 2018.

Editors, A. *Byzantine Empire*. 28 Apr. 2011, www.ancient.eu/Byzantine_Empire/. Accessed 5 July 2018.

Editors, C N. *Mt. Athos: A Visit to the Holy Mountain*. 22 May 2011, www.cbsnews.com/news/mt-athos-a-visit-to-the-holy-mountain/. Accessed 5 July 2018.

Draper, R. *Called to the Holy Mountain*. Dec. 2009, www.nationalgeographic.com/magazine/2009/12/athos/. Accessed 5 July 2018.

Editors, M H. *THE MONKS OF MOUNT ATHOS*. 2018, www.marbleheadsalt.com/the-monks/. Accessed 5 July 2018.

Editors, O W. *Seventh Ecumenical Council*. 27 Nov. 2012, orthodoxwiki.org/Seventh_Ecumenical_Council. Accessed 5 July 2018.

Editors, N W. *Second Council of Nicaea*. 26 Aug. 2015, www.newworldencyclopedia.org/entry/Second_Council_of_Nicaea. Accessed 5 July 2018.

Editors, R. *Battle of Thasos* . 5 May 2018, www.revolvy.com/main/index.php?s=Battle of Thasos. Accessed 5 July 2018.

Kalimniou, D. *The Battle for Arabic Crete*. 25 May 2018, neoskosmos.com/en/116044/the-battle-for-arabic-crete/. Accessed 5 July 2018.

Hendrix, D. *Monasteries of Mount Athos*. 2016, www.thebyzantinelegacy.com/athos. Accessed 5 July 2018.

Editors, V M. *History*. 2015, www.visitmountathos.eu/history.html. Accessed 5 July 2018.

Economidis, N. *The History of Mount Athos During the Byzantine Age*. 2017, www.elpenor.org/athos/en/e21811.asp. Accessed 5 July 2018.

Cartwright, M. *Mount Athos*. 18 Apr. 2018, www.ancient.eu/Mount_Athos/. Accessed 5 July 2018.

Editors, M A. *Athos, Geography and History*. 2013, en.mountathosarea.org/our-area/mount-athos/. Accessed 5 July 2018.

Hendrix, D. *Monastery of the Great Lavra*. 2016, www.thebyzantinelegacy.com/lavra-athos. Accessed 5 July 2018.

Editors, P U. *Rules, Chrysobulls and the Wine Trade on Athos*. 17 Aug. 2014, pemptousia.com/2014/08/rules-chrysobulls-and-the-wine-trade-on-athos/. Accessed 5 July 2018.

Editors, M H. *The Monastery of Megisti Lavra*. 2016, www.macedonian-heritage.gr/Athos/Monastery/Megisti Lavra.html. Accessed 6 July 2018.

Editors, M. *Mount Athos Great Lavra*. 2017, www.monastiria.gr/mount-athos/mount-athos-great-lavra-2/?lang=en. Accessed 6 July 2018.

Posner, D L. *Mount Athos*. Apr. 1964, www.poetryfoundation.org/poetrymagazine/browse?contentId=29716. Accessed 6 July 2018.

Editors, V H. *Mount Athos*. 2018, www.visit-halkidiki.gr/mount-athos/. Accessed 6 July 2018.

Editors, G B. *The "Three Fingers" of the Halkidiki Peninsula*. 2017, www.greekboston.com/travel/halkidiki-peninsula/. Accessed 6 July 2018.

Sanidopoulos, J. *Are Female Animals Forbidden On Mount Athos?* 16 Jan. 2016, www.johnsanidopoulos.com/2016/01/are-female-animals-forbidden-in-mount.html. Accessed 6 July 2018.

Editors, G M. *Apollo*. 2015, www.greekmythology.com/Olympians/Apollo/apollo.html. Accessed 6 July 2018.

Editors, G G. *Apollo and Daphne*. 30 Nov. 2016, greekgodsandgoddesses.net/myths/apollo-and-daphne/. Accessed 6 July 2018.

Sanidopoulos, J. *Alexander the Great, Mount Athos, & a Lofty Proposal*. 30 Apr. 2012, www.johnsanidopoulos.com/2012/04/alexander-great-mount-athos-and-lofty.html. Accessed 6 July 2018.

Editors, O W. *Marcian*. 24 Oct. 2012, orthodoxwiki.org/Marcian. Accessed 6 July 2018.

Džalto, D. *Iconoclastic Controversies*. 2015, www.khanacademy.org/humanities/medieval-world/byzantine1/beginners-guide-byzantine/a/iconoclastic-controversies. Accessed 6 July 2018.

Beşliu, P. *The Archaeology of the Medieval Towers in Mount Athos. An Attempt of Archaeological Research*. 28 Jan. 2011, revistatransilvania.ro/wp-content/uploads/2018/02/12.Muntean.pdf. Accessed 6 July 2018.

Editors, O W. *Canon (Hymn)*. 12 Aug. 2009, orthodoxwiki.org/Canon_(hymn). Accessed 6 July 2018.

Appleton, R. *Mount Athos*. 2007, www.newadvent.org/cathen/02047b.htm. Accessed 6 July 2018.

Editors, R. *Protos (Monastic Office)* . 31 Jan. 2018, www.revolvy.com/topic/Protos-(monastic-office). Accessed 6 July 2018.

Editors, E B. *Saint Athanasius the Athonite*. 17 Apr. 2015, www.britannica.com/biography/Saint-Athanasius-the-Athonite. Accessed 6 July 2018.

Editors, O W. *Mount Athos*. 9 May 2016, orthodoxwiki.org/Mount_Athos. Accessed 6 July 2018.

Editors, O W. *Athanasius of Athos*. 22 Oct. 2012, orthodoxwiki.org/Athanasius_of_Athos. Accessed 9 July 2018.

Editors, D I. *A ROMANO-BYZANTINE INSTITUTE*. 2018, dialogos-institute.org/?byzantium. Accessed 9 July 2018.

Editors, R. *Second Council of Lyon*. 9 Mar. 2018, www.revolvy.com/main/index.php?s=Second Council of Lyon. Accessed 9 July 2018.

Editors, O W. *Zographou Monastery (Athos)*. 8 Jan. 2011, orthodoxwiki.org/Zographou_Monastery_(Athos). Accessed 9 July 2018.

Editors, E N. *'Not an Anthologist: John Bekkos as a Reader of the Fathers.'* 30 Oct. 2009, eirenikon.wordpress.com/2009/10/30/not-an-anthologist-john-bekkos-as-a-reader-of-the-fathers/. Accessed 9 July 2018.

Editors, R. *Gregory of Sinai* . 10 Jan. 2018, www.revolvy.com/main/index.php?s=Gregory of Sinai. Accessed 9 July 2018.

Editors, R. *Gregory Palamas*. 20 June 2018, www.revolvy.com/main/index.php?s=Gregory Palamas. Accessed 9 July 2018.

Editors, W S. *Catholic Encyclopedia (1913)/Mount Athos*. 6 Feb. 2012, en.wikisource.org/wiki/Catholic_Encyclopedia_(1913)/Mount_Athos. Accessed 9 July 2018.

Rentoulas, A. *Fasting and Feasting on Mount Athos*. 12 July 2016, www.greece-is.com/mt-athos-monastic-diet-food-soul/. Accessed 9 July 2018.

Editors, M H. *The Monastery of Konstamonitou*. 2017, www.macedonian-heritage.gr/Athos/Monastery/Konstamonitou.html. Accessed 9 July 2018.

Editors, P U. *The Holy Monastery of Koutloumousiou*. 5 Nov. 2011, pemptousia.com/2011/11/the-holy-monastery-of-koutloumousiou/. Accessed 9 July 2018.

Editors, M H. *The Monastery of Gregoriou*. 2017, www.macedonian-heritage.gr/Athos/Monastery/Gregoriou.html. Accessed 9 July 2018.

Editors, M. *Pantocrator Monastery*. 2017, www.monastiria.gr/mount-athos/mount-athos-pantocrators-monastery/?lang=en. Accessed 9 July 2018.

Hendrix, D. *Pantokrator Monastery*. 2016, www.thebyzantinelegacy.com/pantokrator-athos. Accessed 9 July 2018.

Editors, O W. *Council of Florence*. 7 Nov. 2011, orthodoxwiki.org/Council_of_Florence. Accessed 9 July 2018.

Liester, M B. *Hesychasm: A Christian Path of Transcendence*. 2000, www.theosophical.org/publications/1432. Accessed 9 July 2018.

Katz, N. *How Do Mount Athos Monks Stay so Healthy?* 8 Dec. 2011, www.cbsnews.com/news/how-do-mount-athos-monks-stay-so-healthy/. Accessed 9 July 2018.

Editors, V M. *Daily Life*. 2017, www.visitmountathos.eu/daily-life.html. Accessed 9 July 2018.

Tzimas, S. *A Monk Shares His Love of God, Food and Wine.* 7 Feb. 2016, www.ekathimerini.com/210035/article/ekathimerini/life/a-monk-shares-his-love-of-god-food-and-wine. Accessed 9 July 2018.

Ellis, J. *THE MYSTERIOUS MONKS OF MOUNT ATHOS.* 29 May 2016, www.jamesellisfitness.com/mysterious-monks-mount-athos/. Accessed 9 July 2018.

Editors, H M. *MONKS AND RITUALS OF DAILY LIFE.* 2017, holymountain.omeka.net/exhibits/show/holy-mountain/monks-and-rituals-of-daily-lif. Accessed 9 July 2018.

Editors, M. *Mount Athos Monastery of Gregoriou.* 2015, www.monastiria.gr/mount-athos/mount-athos-monastery-of-grigoriou/?lang=en. Accessed 9 July 2018.

Flynn, D. *Monastic Mount Athos Offers a Glimpse Back in Time.* 13 Nov. 2008, www.reuters.com/article/us-greece-athos/monastic-mount-athos-offers-a-glimpse-back-in-time-idUSTRE4AC3RY20081113. Accessed 9 July 2018.

Mantzaridis, G. *The Monastic Life: The Way of Perfection.* 27 Apr. 2015, pemptousia.com/2015/04/the-monastic-life-the-way-of-perfection-the-holy-mount-athos/. Accessed 9 July 2018.

Editors, V W. *Secrets of the World's Healthiest People: Mount Athos Monks – Part 1 Diet.* 12 Sept. 2015, vibrantliveswellbeing.com/the-worlds-healthiest-people-mount-athos-monks-part-1-diet/. Accessed 9 July 2018.

Editors, M A. *Mount Athos Sketes.* 2017, mountathos-eshop.com/en/mount-athos-true-guardian-greek-orthodoxy/mount-athos-sketes/. Accessed 9 July 2018.

Chrysochoidis, K. *Cells, Sketes, and Monasteries in Mt Athos' History.* 26 Feb. 2016, pemptousia.com/2016/02/32974/. Accessed 9 July 2018.

Editors, S R. *Traditional Skull Painting Practiced by the Monks on Mount Athos.* 8 Mar. 2014, strangeremains.com/2014/03/08/traditional-skull-painting-of-mt-athos-in-greece/. Accessed 9 July 2018.

Editors, C D. *The Burial Practices on Mt. Athos.* 28 Dec. 2017, blog.obitel-minsk.com/2017/12/the-burial-practices-on-mt-athos.html. Accessed 9 July 2018.

Editors, A O. *Hermitages of Karoulia.* 2018, www.atlasobscura.com/places/hermitages-of-karoulia. Accessed 9 July 2018.

Editors, M. *The Jesus Prayer*. 2015, www.monastiriaka.gr/en/the-jesus-prayer-n-92301.html. Accessed 9 July 2018.

Lockard, J. *Holy Misogyny*. 24 May 2011, souciant.com/2011/05/holy-misogyny/. Accessed 9 July 2018.

Chrysopoulos, P. *Aliki Diplarakou: Greece's First 'Miss Europe.'* 8 Feb. 2018, greece.greekreporter.com/2018/02/08/aliki-diplarakou-greeces-first-miss-europe/. Accessed 9 July 2018.

Romer, F. E. (Ed.). (1998). *Pomponius Mela's Description of the World*. University of Michigan Press.

Chupungco, A. J. (2016). *Handbook for Liturgical Studies, Volume V: Liturgical Time and Space*(Vol. V). Liturgical Press.

Herrin, J. (2008). *Byzantium: The Surprising Life of a Medieval Empire*. Penguin UK.

Bryer, A., & Cunningham, M. (2016). *Mount Athos and Byzantine Monasticism: Papers from the Twenty-Eighth Spring Symposium of Byzantine Studies, University of Birmingham*. Routledge.

Free Books by Charles River Editors

We have brand new titles available for free most days of the week. To see which of our titles are currently free, click on this link.

Discounted Books by Charles River Editors

We have titles at a discount price of just 99 cents everyday. To see which of our titles are currently 99 cents, click on this link.

CPSIA information can be obtained
at www.ICGtesting.com
Printed in the USA
LVHW021329020622
720304LV00008B/532